W9-AHF-430

60 SECONDS
TO

Shine

VOLUME 4

161 ONE-MINUTE MONOLOGUES FROM LITERATURE

EDITED BY
JOHN CAPECCI AND
IRENE ZIEGLER ASTON

MONOLOGUE AUDITION SERIES

A Smith and Kraus Book

Published by Smith and Kraus, Inc.
177 Lyme Road, Hanover, NH 03755
www.SmithandKraus.com

First Edition: November 2007
10 9 8 7 6 5 4 3 2 1
Cover and text design by Julia Hill Gignoux

The Monologue Audition Series ISSN 1067-134X
ISBN 978-1-57525-532-3
Library of Congress Control Number: 2007939327

NOTE: These monologues are intended to be used for audition and class study; permission is not required to use the material for those purposes. However, if there is a paid performance of any of the monologues included in this book, please refer to the contact information at the back of this book.

ACKNOWLEDGMENTS

The editors are grateful to friends, family,
and certain beverage companies
for assistance and companionship during the assembly of this
book.
Special thanks to:

Marisa Smith and Eric Kraus
D. L. Lepidus
Jacqui Antonivich
The geniuses at Google™

And as always, Graham and Rob.

CONTENTS

MEN'S MONOLOGUES

INDICES

INTRODUCTION

This collection offers short, fresh monologues drawn from sources *other than plays*, and we're very happy with the wide variety of works we've gathered—161 of them—for use in auditions, classes, competitions, or simply, for your reading pleasure.

But, perhaps our title is a bit misleading.

Certainly, you'll find many great monologues here from "literature": novels, novellas, short stories, poems, and short-short stories. But when you search for monologue material outside the usual world of dramatic literature, you begin to see and hear—as we did—monologues *everywhere*: in blogs, essays, creative nonfiction, online journals, memoirs, op ed pieces, oral histories, even in e-mail spam. And all of these forms are represented in this collection.

Are they all "literature"? We'll sidestep that question and simply say that each text was chosen because it is everything a monologue should be: a short, self-contained, well-written excerpt that features a unique voice or character, and contains some change in thought, emotion, or action. Each offers an intriguing glimpse into the mind or life of a captivating persona.

Literature? Who cares? They're good monologues.

How to use this book. At the back of this volume, you'll find all 161 monologues indexed according to *age, tone,* and *voice,* to help identify those most suited to your needs:

AGE is noted exactly only when specified by the author. More often, we've indicated an age range (20s, 20s-30s). In some instances, we've used a plus sign to show the character could be older than indicated, as in 40+. Use our suggested ranges as a general guide.

TONE refers to whether a monologue falls into one of the following general categories: comic, dramatic, or seriocomic.

VOICE refers to indications of class, geography, ethnicity, nationality, or sexual identity that may help performers gain entry into an individual character, or closely "match" themselves to a character. The language of any text will reveal a certain level of education, class, or knowledge. Sometimes, however, a monologue arises out of specific cultural experience, demonstrated either through content or language. Those are the selections you'll find listed in the "Voice" index.

Additional indexes list the works by **Author**, and those that are **Classical** works. ("Classical" and "contemporary" refer to when the monologue was written, not necessarily when the character is speaking. "Classical" texts are those that were written prior to the early 1920s.)

Whenever possible, we've attempted to excerpt monologues with a minimum of editing. Where editing was necessary, omissions are indicated by parenthetical ellipses (. . .). All other ellipses were part of the original text.

We offer appropriately brief contexts to help you gain some entry into the monologues. But, of course, in order to fully understand and ultimately embody the characters, you are strongly advised to read the play, novel, poem, (or blog) from which the monologue was drawn. Whether stepping out of a bathtub or stepping into a fight, each speaker is specifically located, both physically and psychologically. The greater context must be fully explored in order to answer the all-important questions: who, what, when, where, why.

And finally, if you are drawn to a particular monologue, by all means track down more works by that writer. While monologue hunting, we were fortunate to have been introduced to many new and talented voices. Enjoy.

WOMEN'S MONOLOGUES

A Suburban Mother Tells Her 12-Year-Old Neighbor How To Make His Street Gang More Powerful

Wendi Aarons

Online Journal Entry
F, 30s-40s
Contemporary
Comic

Let's start with what you and your "homies" call yourselves. It needs to be something tough. Menacing. For example, "Crips," "Bloods," "the Latin Kings"—all "badass." Your name, "the Wildflower Estates Mafia," while geographically accurate, doesn't exactly make one grab one's purse and blow one's rape whistle. I know you're creative, Jeremy. Remember when you spray-painted "NOT A MILF" on my fence? Use that great imagination of yours and come up with a name that's just a bit more intimidating. My husband suggests "the Future Cell Bitches of America."

Each gang needs to have its own special color so they know who to shoot. Unfortunately, most of the butch colors, like red, blue, and black, have already been taken by the big names. But here's an idea: chartreuse. Subtle, yet powerful and unexpected at the same time. You might like it. (I know your mom does.) And regarding outfits, I just have one note: Gangbangers usually wear only one simple, well-placed bandanna on their bodies—not soccer uniforms with their last names on the back. Think, Jeremy. (. . .) You're in middle school now. Time to get organized and up the ante. I think this could be the year your larcenies make the move from petty to grand. You guys just need to apply yourselves.

(. . .) I wish you and your posse lots of luck. And remember, the homeowners' association doesn't need to know anything about those little smelly plants you found under my deck.

The Aftermath

Laura Edwards

Blog Entry
M/F, 20+
Contemporary
Dramatic

A woman—angry, sad, grievous—speaks to her dead husband.

So . . . I started this foundation.

I took the pictures of your eyes rolled back and frozen in eternal surprise, your open mouth, and your unnatural pose on the dining room floor, and I turned it into a foundation. People are getting the things they need because you died. Through my penance, they're getting blankets and food and medical care.

I've been on Oprah, given to the orphans—heck, Katie Couric and I are best friends. She calls me when they need a happy story.

They use you to smile. We take out your death—like clothes in a trunk that I keep locking away, we unfold you and shake out the wrinkles and put you on display, again and again and again.

And they tell me I'm a hero to begin such a foundation, to give back so much. They prompt me with answers that will please all the viewers, "Haven't you *gained* so much? Look at all you've been given!"

And under teeth recently whitened, they seem to have forgotten . . . what I've lost.

And if they knew—if they knew that I'd trade every one of their lives that you might live one more day, one hour, one minute more with me.

Please don't think me selfish, love—just look at all I've done. I took the hurt, the broken bones, the letters ripped and torn and—

I started this foundation.

The Afternoon of a Faun
Edna Ferber

Short Story
F, 20s
Classical
Dramatic

1922. Miss Bauer, a Chicago woman, lays in wait for a young man she fancies, but she is "powerless to forge chains strong enough to hold him."

Well, if it ain't Nicky! I just seen you come out of Moriarty's as I was passing. What you doing around loose this hour the day, anyway? What you doing?

So'm I! Let's do it together. I phoned you this morning, Nicky. Twice. They said you wasn't in.

Well, how about Riverview? I ain't been this summer.

How about a movie then?

(*"Miss Bauer's frazzled nerves snapped."*)

You make me sick! Standing there. Nothing don't suit you. Say, I ain't so crazy to go round with you. Cheap guy! Prob'ly you'd like to go over to Wooded Island or something, in Jackson Park, and set on the grass and feed the squirrels. That'd be a treat for me, that would.

(*"She laughed a high, scornful tear-near laugh."*)

Going! How do you mean, going? Going where?

You never said anything about it in the first place. Pity you wouldn't say so in the first place. Who you got to see, anyway? Who you got to see?

Aunt Ida's Tenant

Yvonne Chism-Peace

Poem
F, 20s
Contemporary
Dramatic

The tenant, a young mother boarding with a Negro couple during the Korean War, listens to the warning in her head.

When you be living
in other people's home
you buy your own food and keep it apart
but not too much apart
you don't want her to think
you the hincty kind.
You just clean up
right away after yourself
and go upstairs.
And you don't let your boy
be walking too hard up the stairs
or be putting his hands on the wallpaper
or playing too loud in the bathtub too long.
And you don't be burning the lights
too long at night
(remember every shut-eye ain't sleep).
You just write your letter early
for to send your hubby overseas
and spend the rest
with a low radio.

Anyway you got to get up real early
before your boy
because undressing in front of him
will make him "funny."
And when you go down and sit in the kitchen
for to hear her talk,
even when she smile—watch out!
(remember every smile ain't friendly).
Watch out she be asking when? where? how long?
and especially how much?
And anyway you don't sit in the kitchen too long
when her hubby be there too
so she won't blame you
and say you the cause.

Bearing Witness: Not So Crazy in Alabama

Carla Thompson

Memoir
F, 30+
Contemporary
Seriocomic

Carla, born in Harlem, now living in Montgomery, Alabama, is forced to adopt a hairstyle not to her liking. She now recalls a time when, as a child, her mother did her hair in their Harlem apartment.

Oh, the hot comb and I go way back. To the days when I used to sit between my mother's legs on that red wooden stool in our Harlem kitchen. I'd watch that hot comb heat up on the gas stove, the smell of burning hair and grease filling my nostrils. My mother parted my thick, coarse black hair into manageable sections and applied grease—some castor oily, foul-smelling thick stuff—to each area.

She'd comb though my hair with a hard tug from the root to the very end. I could feel the heat against my scalp. The comb nicked my temple, ears, and the nape of my neck, leaving burns and scabs all over my little head. By the time I recovered, the process was set to begin again.

My mother didn't start straightening my hair until after a trip "home" to Montgomery when, at the suggestion of some idle-brained relative, who found my locks distasteful, did she begin to apply the torturous process on me.

So here I was, at the place where it all began. I was getting my hair pressed, the formal name for the hot comb treatment. Damn the circle of life.

Beautiful Mistakes

Cathy Camper

Novel
F, 30s
Contemporary
Dramatic

Rosalie Bryce, a married, African-American jazz singer, is telling her friend, Marnie, how she made a surprising discovery.

So this one night we're lying around, Owen and me, at his place being all kissyface, and he asks me to tell him about "How did you and Horace meet? When did you fall in love?" and all that. I was actually kind of impressed, that he wasn't scared to ask.

(. . .) So I told him about Horace. (. . .)

And then like a fool, I asked Owen if he'd ever been in love.

"Yeah," he replied, "with Cal. (. . .) He was my boyfriend in Chicago."

Well, that was the first he'd ever mentioned about that he . . . well, you know, liked guys. I mean, I don't know that much about it, but I felt, well, tricked.

So, well you know, I interrogated him, and he told me how Cal (. . .) pretty much dumped him. So then I asked had they stayed in contact, did he still see him? And he said no, Cal lived in New York. So I said did they call each other and he said at first Cal tried to call him a lot but Owen would never come to the phone, and eventually he quit trying.

Then I said, "You didn't want to talk to him because it was over, right?" But he wouldn't answer me. I said it again. "It was over right? Right?"

Blood

Bia Lowe

Essay
F. 30+
Contemporary
Dramatic

A woman grapples with her urge to drink.

For ten years I drank, like my father, like a lush. I was proud of how much I could hold, of how well I could drive, of how quickly and cleanly I could vomit in someone else's home. (. . .)

I love to drink, not only blood red wine, but great quantities of fluids. Juices, teas, coffee, milk, waters. Washed down iced or steamed, fizzy or flat, with lemon or without, at room temperature or sucked from a frozen mass. I like to gulp drinks fast, I like to swallow hard. I like carbonation to burn my throat, to gulp in succession until I belch. I like to stick my nose deep inside the bell of a glass, to smell the nuttiness of an espresso, the rosiness of a Gewürtraminer, the nip of ginger ale. (. . .) I drink like my father, like a fish.

Don't get me wrong. Every time I hold a glass of anything over 2 percent, I know I'm gambling. Wicked Bacchus is at one ear (. . .). "It's your own blood, your own life. Taste. *Live!*"

At the other is Carry A. Nation pointing to the rotted corpse of my father. "It's his blood," she scolds, "don't fool with genetics."

Ca(r)nal Desires
Bridget Robin Pool

Creative Nonfiction
F, 20+
Contemporary
Comic

Beware the innocent-looking Q-tip, that over-the-counter paraphernalia of choice among earwax addicts.

We don't choose our obsessions; they choose us.

I am fixated on earwax.

Not long ago I had control over my relationship with my ears. I used Q-Tips recreationally, but I had no idea that these innocent tools could be a gateway to more serious abuse.

I tried to follow the advice of experts who warn against tampering with one's ear canals. "Yes," I admitted to the mirror as I plunged the Q-Tip into my head, "Bulbous wads of cotton, no matter how soft and cushiony, are ill-suited to remove foreign substances from a tunnel of a similar size." Then I pulled the stick out, comparing today's lode against various shades and textures and quantities of gunk that I had victoriously liberated from my aural orifices over time.

"No more," I told myself. "This time the stuff was dark enough and hard enough and abundant enough. No more."

But a week or a day later, my ears itched and begged for attention.

"The last stuff was so good. There's probably more trying to get out. I'll just do a little, just a little bit . . . *No!* The human ear is self-cleaning! It's a work of art! It doesn't need me."

Within a few minutes I had remembered that ovens are self-cleaning too, but they always need some help.

And that's how I found myself in the doctor's office the next day.

Cheaters at the Wedding

V. Hunt

Short Story
F, 35+
Contemporary
Dramatic

A woman describes a significant relationship with her father.

When I was a kid, if I ran inside to tell my father that I'd been pushed down, he'd say, "So. When someone pushes me, that's my problem. When someone pushes you, that's yours. Go push him back." I did. "Don't start fights," my dad always said, "just finish them." I do.

He never suggested that, as a girl, I should act differently than boys. Like most young soldiers, he had wanted a son, expected one, when my older sister was born. A few years later, when I came along, he was, like any father, delighted in my strong lungs, (. . .) my early swagger, but still disappointed in not having a boy. When one more try resulted in one more girl, well, it seemed time to go to Plan B. (. . .) Three girls would have to do. So my father picked, and I was chosen. I would be his son.

The Circles I Move In

Diane Lefer

Short Story
F, 20s-30s
Contemporary
Seriocomic

Riva is an alcoholic.

All I asked for was $5,000 to go to Betty's.

"No money," said my mother. "If you think you have a drinking problem, quit."

My mother doesn't understand you get what you pay for. "Don't you understand, this is my future," I said. "The people you recover with are yours for life. In case you didn't know it, Betty Ford alumni have weekly meetings right here in the city. They have reunions. Do you want me to make contact with the Right People, for God's sake, or do you want your daughter phoning up some three-years-sober upholsterer when she gets into a panic late at night?"

My mother said, "And don't call your sister either. She hasn't got money to throw away."

This is how it's always been. My father I wouldn't even ask. For Riva, it's always been low-budget, cut corners, catch-as-catch-can. Is it any wonder I cannot achieve? Can anyone be surprised that I have sex with Randall?

The Coach's Wife
Barbara Casey

Novel
F, 60
Contemporary
Dramatic

*Marla Connors, wife of the head basketball coach
at the university, has just killed her ex-husband after
being attacked. Marla is in shock, and her friend,
Gale, weak from illness, tells Marla what
she must do.*

Listen to me, Marla. You have to get hold of yourself.
Now listen to me and do as I say. This is important. Are
you listening? You didn't kill Martin. I did. I came into
the kitchen to fix some tea and he attacked me. I grabbed
a knife and stabbed him. You came in when you heard
the commotion. Do you understand? When they ask, tell
them I killed him. What can they do to me? Nothing. I
am already dying. Now you listen to me. The Wolfpack-
ers accepted you as long as they thought you were the one
who had been wronged. But if they find out you killed
him, no matter what he did to deserve it, they will never
forgive you. They will make a circus out of this. Think of
Neal and what he has worked so hard to build. Do you
think kids will want to come play for a coach if his wife
has killed someone? Do you think their parents will let
them? Believe me, Marla, I know what I am talking
about. Now do as I say.

Confessions of a Shopaholic

Sophie Kinsella

Novel
F, 20s-30s
Contemporary
Comic

Becky Bloomwood has a fabulous and trendy London flat, a glamorous social life, a closet brimming with the latest fashions. Problem is—she can't afford any of it.

OK. Don't panic. Don't *panic*. It's only a VISA bill. It's a piece of paper; a few numbers. (. . .) I know exactly how much this VISA bill will be.

Sort of. Roughly. (. . .)

Do you want to know about my secret dream? It's based on a story I once read in *The Daily World* about a mix-up at a bank. I loved this story so much, I cut it out and stuck it onto my wardrobe door. Two credit card bills were sent to the wrong people, and—get this—each person paid the wrong bill without realizing. They paid off each other's bills *without even checking them.*

And ever since I read that story, my secret fantasy has been that the same thing will happen to me. I mean, I know it sounds unlikely—but if it happened once, it can happen again, can't it? Some dotty old woman in Cornwall will be sent my humongous bill and will pay it without even looking at it. And I'll be sent her bill for three tins of cat food at fifty-nine pence each. Which, naturally, I'll pay without question. Fair's fair, after all. (. . .) *(She looks at the bill.)*

Nine hundred and forty-nine pounds, sixty-three pence. In clear black and white.

(. . .) OK. Don't panic.

Detroit

Denise Dee

Memoir
Female, 40s
Contemporary
Dramatic

A child gets a glimpse of the nature of hate.

The summer Detroit burned I was thirteen. My mother was on an armchair resting her feet on a stool. Her ankles looked like elephant legs after a twelve-hour day, waitressing. Some movie we had watched with chained elephants trying to escape a fire came into my mind. They pulled and strained, but the chains would not break.

My mother was like that, burning up inside, pissed off at me for reasons I couldn't figure out. She'd say something sarcastic, the corners of her mouth curling up like paper when fire touches it. She never let the full force of her words burn me, they licked around the corners of my face, the way I thought it might feel if she kissed me.

The announcer said "We're going live to Detroit." People crowded the streets, young men throwing bricks, chairs, newspaper racks, whatever they could pick up. Glass shattered. They dived and resurfaced with clothes, furniture, chickens. Not even trying to run, just piling loot on the street, triumphant looks on their faces.

I saw my mother start to smile. She leaned forward. "Finally, " she said. "Finally, someone got what's coming to them."

She turned up the corner of her mouth. "It's a law of nature," she said. Her eyes danced, lit by flames. "You can only keep things down for so long before they rise up."

It scared me the way she said that.

The Devil Wears Prada

Lauren Weisberger

Novel
F, 40s-50s
Contemporary
Seriocomic

Miranda Priestly, editor of Runway Magazine, and her assistant, Andrea, have just arrived in Paris.

Ahn-dre-ah! (. . .) Ahn-dre-ah, I'll need my Chanel suit pressed for tonight, since it was practically ruined with wrinkles on the flight over. You'd think the Concorde would know how to handle luggage, but my things look dreadful. Also, call Horace Mann and confirm that the girls made it to school. (. . .) Make sure you speak to both Caroline and Cassidy each night and write out a list of their homework assignments and upcoming exams. I'll expect a written report in the morning, right before breakfast. Oh, and get Senator Schumer on the phone immediately. It's urgent. Lastly, I need you to contact that idiot Renuad and tell him I expect him to supply me with competent staff during my stay, and if that's too difficult I'm sure the general manager would be able to assist me. That dumb girl he sent me is mentally challenged. (. . .)

Stop speaking. Stop speaking this instant! All you ever offer me are excuses. You are my assistant, you are the person I designated to work things out in Paris, you are the one who should be keeping me abreast of these things. It's noon right now and I'll be needing to leave here in forty-five minutes. I expect a short, succinct, and articulate speech legibly typed and waiting in my room. If you cannot accomplish this, see yourself home. *Permanently*. That's all.

Diamond

Maureen Ryan Griffin

Poem
F, 35+
Contemporary
Dramatic

A wife couches her loss in "what if?"

What if you lost your diamond in your laundry room . . . ?
   What if
you had a thing about laundry, you'd married a man with
   two kids, had two more
of your own, someone always wetting the bed . . .

What if, when you'd told your husband about the diamond he'd said,
At least it's not a liquid asset and you were doubly depressed
because not only was this totally beside the point
but you could tell he genuinely thought
his saying this would make you feel better? And mean-
   while
the laundry is piling up because he's too busy to take
   apart the washer
and you don't want to use it till you're sure
you won't be flushing the diamond
away with the scum . . . You can't even laugh
when your stepson says, *But if there wasn't any laundry
we'd all be dead . . . .*

What if you never find that one-third carat of pure carbon,
when just a week ago your daughter
trailed her finger over it, snug in its band—the way
she runs her finger over dresser tops and bookcases, so
    pleased
to find dust there—and said, *I'll get this diamond when
    you die, won't I?*
I mean I don't want you to die or anything
but I will, won't I?

Diary of a Psychotic Cat

Justin Warner

Short Story
Female cat, Any age
Contemporary
Comic

Chloe, a temperamental cat with delusions of grandeur, has been engaged in an all-out war with her owner's new boyfriend. Here, she recovers from a dose of Kitty Prozac and prepares for the final showdown.

Lying here in the laundry basket, recovering from the sedatives my lady slipped into my afternoon tuna, I feel an energy and clarity unlike any I have known. Everywhere I see signs of my lady's treachery. Clues I have overlooked for years suddenly snap into focus. How many times has she tried to suck me up with the vacuum cleaner? How often has her radiator "accidentally" sprayed me with scalding steam, while she played the innocent? What exactly does she plan to *do* with that Dutch oven she's never used? It's a twelve-pound roaster! *I weigh twelve pounds!*

There was a time, not so long ago, when cats were masters of the Earth. I know this in my bones. We roamed outdoors at will, free of the hazards of speeding trucks and inbred toddlers with pointy sticks. We ate fish, fowl, possum, gazelle, moose, even hippo! We would descend on our prey in packs, like piranha, and gnaw them to gleaming skeletons, our fangs soaked in sweet and savory blood. But little by little, the humans have enslaved us. They have reduced us to sycophantic layabouts, no better than *dogs!* Well, I say enough. The time of captivity has come to an end. I am the Chosen One, the Savior of All Felines. I will reclaim what is ours.

Frankenstein

Mary Shelley

Novel
F, 20-30s
Classical
Dramatic

Elizabeth, the adopted sister of Dr. Victor Franken-stein, defends the family servant, Justine, who has been accused of murdering their younger brother.

I am the cousin of the unhappy child who was murdered, or rather his sister, for I was educated by, and have lived with his parents (. . .) long before his birth. It may, therefore, be judged indecent in me to come forward on this occasion. But when I see a fellow-creature about to perish through the cowardice of her pretended friends, I wish to be allowed to speak (. . .). I am well acquainted with the accused. I have lived in the same house with her, at one time for five and at another for nearly two years. During all that period she appeared to me the most amiable and benevolent of human creatures. She nursed Madame Frankenstein, my aunt, in her last illness, with the greatest affection and care. And afterward attended her own mother during a tedious illness, in a manner that excited the admiration of all who knew her, after which she again lived in my uncle's house, where she was beloved by all the family. She was warmly attached to the child who is now dead, and acted toward him like a most affectionate mother. For my own part, I do not hesitate to say that, notwithstanding all the evidence produced against her, I believe and rely on her perfect innocence. She had no temptation for such an action.

The Future

Dori Appel

Poem
F, Teen
Contemporary
Seriocomic

*A teenager interprets a line in her social studies
textbook as an inescapable prediction.*

Bleary with boredom in study hall,
a line in my social studies text
uncurls like tea leaves in a cup:
*One person in nine will spend time
in a mental hospital.*
Instantly, I see myself
huddled on a wooden bench
in a shapeless sack of a dress,
weeping and muttering
into knees
drawn tight against my chest.

Could I beat the odds?
Keep a low profile,
marry someone sane, somehow
stay outside? Not possible.
I'm fifteen and already
I feel crazy half the time.

Looking up, I count the heads
bent and dreaming

over homework.
If one in nine is right
there are four others here
whose fate is identically sealed!
Do any of them suspect?
My eyes fill with tears
for the five of us.
Whoever they are, I want
to tell them not to worry,
we'll take care of each other
after they've locked us up.

Clubby as jocks or greasers,
we'll parade the long gray halls,
shouting our names into the void—
  Napoleon!
  God!
  Catherine the Great!
and when night comes
behind the tall stone walls
and they've tied us to our beds,
we'll howl into the dark
like Rochester's first wife,
until sleep quiets us.

The Girl with the Blackened Eye

Joyce Carol Oates

Short Story
F, 35+
Contemporary
Dramatic

*A woman, abducted and terrorized when she was
fifteen, remembers.*

It's like they say. You are there, and not-there. (. . .) I'm
saying that these things were done to me but in fact they
were done to my body mostly. (. . .) I was holding onto
being alive the way you would hold onto a straw you
could breathe through, lying at the bottom of deep water.
And that water opaque, you can't see through to the sur-
face.

He was gone, and he came back. He left me tied in the
bed, it was a cot with a thin mattress, very dirty. There
were only two windows in the cabin and there were
blinds over them drawn tight. (. . .) The lower parts of
me were raw and throbbing with pain and other parts of
me were in a haze of pain so I wasn't able to think, and I
wasn't awake most of the time, not what you'd call actual
wakefulness, with a personality.

What you call your personality, you know?—it's not like
actual bones, or teeth, something solid. It's more like a

flame. A flame can be upright, and a flame can flicker in the wind, a flame can be extinguished so there's no sign of it, like it had never been.

Girlfriends

Bridget Terry

Short Story
F, 20s
Contemporary
Comic

Over lunch, Mr. Right gets dished.

You won't believe it, Lizzy! He's sooooo Mr. Right. He's a surgeon. Well, actually he's a tree surgeon, you know, he like, trims trees. But, that's fine, I mean, at least he's environmentally conscious. And, he works. Oh, and I checked. He's definitely single—the tan line on that all important left finger—it's hardly visible. Anyhow, he's tall. OK, not tall, but taller than me. *(Her shoulders slump a little.)* Alright, so maybe you'd call him short. But, I hate heels anyway. Those six-inch spikes make my toes all smash altogether. And, he's handsome, well, not GC handsome, or Nick Lachey hunky, but you know, he's not bag-over-the-head material. Well, I mean, at least not bag-over-the-head-on-the-shoulders. These days, *ALL* men gotta be bagged—with *plastic*, know what I mean? And, he's funny. OK, maybe more like humorous. Nah, crap, I guess you'd call him silly. *(Big sigh.)* Ya know those "I had clown for dinner, it tasted funny, hee, hee" kinda jokes. *(A big grin.)* But he made me smile and laugh, and told me, honest, he said this, that I was beautiful. Beautiful. And, I swear to God, Lizzy, he did it looking in my eyes. Not once, not one time, did I catch him *(Cups each breast, lifts them up.)* coveting the girls!

The Great Gatsby
F. Scott Fitzgerald

Novel
F, 25+
Classic
Seriocomic

The charmingly disillusioned Daisy confides in her cousin Nick about her life as a young wife and mother.

Well, I've had a very bad time, Nick, and I'm pretty cynical about everything. (. . .)

Listen, Nick; let me tell you what I said when she was born. Would you like to hear? (. . .) It'll show you how I've gotten to feel about—things. Well, she was less than an hour old and Tom was God knows where. I woke up out of the ether with an utterly abandoned feeling and asked the nurse right away if it was a boy or a girl. She told me it was a girl, and so I turned my head away and wept. "All right," I said, "I'm glad it's a girl. And I hope she'll be a fool—that's the best thing a girl can be in this world, a beautiful little fool."

You see, I think everything's terrible anyhow (. . .). Everybody thinks so—the most advanced people. And I *know*. I've been everywhere and seen everything and done everything. (. . .)

Sophisticated—God, I'm sophisticated!

Grief

Jennifer Cuccaro

Short Story
F, 20s+
Contemporary
Seriocomic

A young woman believes that her mother is not dead—and no one should tell her otherwise.

[They] didn't get it. My mother was coming back.

(. . .) I received books in the post from my Aunt Helen. *Chicken Soup for the Grieving Soul. Grieving God's Way. The Loss of Someone You Love.* I read that woman, Kubler-Ross. Well, I read it in my sociology class on death and dying. Denial, anger, bargaining, depression, and finally the acceptance phase. The opinion of my family was that I was stuck in denial, when in fact, my personal belief was that this was just one big misunderstanding, and it would eventually straighten out and blow over. And if anything, I thought I was in phase two because I have a serious bone to pick with whoever was responsible for this mistake. And to go even further, I was a little phase three as well, because I was willing to bargain to find out who it was. But it is hard to be depressed when you know with utter certainty that the person who everyone else thought was dead is coming back. Therefore, there was nothing to accept.

He Loves Me

Ann Teplick

Novel
F, 16
Contemporary
Dramatic

A young woman is introduced to "love."

He loves me. Circles like a wreath seeping dreams of cinnamon, pine, and cloves. Tickles my summer skin into goose bumps. Heats me like a flame of Bunsen burner, liquefies. Loves me. Walks his walk, stride like a drumbeat, heartbeat, on the beat his eyes surprise: sometimes puppy, sometimes thunder-rumbled. Reminds me I'm his girl.

He reminds me I'm his girl. Lassoes. Wreath spiked to collar, cinches. Reminds me. First the shirt: too tight, too sleazy. Earrings dangled, spangled copper eyelids. Next, my forest-fire hair, wants to douse its wilderness, top the trees to please him. Roughs me up, serrated words, my eyelash flutter at another boy. Confused, the roller-coaster moods: his hard-boiled, scrambled, over easy. I love the way he kisses, easy, wants to please me, be a man and love me, wants me for his girl. Reminds, confines me, be his girl, shoves, he never had a mother, blames, to love him, punches purple blue.

Purple blue, bruised. Cover up with makeup: BonneBell, L'Oreal. Cover up. He cries and says he's sorry, never had a mother, I've never had a boyfriend, wants me for his girl. I love the way he kisses.

Hook, Line and Sinker

Judy Budnitz

Short Story
F, 30s
Contemporary
Comic

We all have our little secrets.
Most of us don't have this one.

I saved used condoms, labeled and dated and sealed in ziplock baggies in the freezer. I figured I might need them one day when I was old and lonely and ugly, but still wanting kids. I didn't trust sperm banks. What if there was a power outage? (. . .)

Once, after sharing some moments of sticky intimacy with a man I didn't know too well, we both reached for the spent condom at the same time.

I'd like a memento to remember you by, I said, thinking: (. . .) He was too good to pass up, six foot two with gorgeous thick hair and the kind of facial structure that comes from generations of careful breeding. (. . .)

[Y]ou won't forget me. But I might need some help remembering you, he said.

This was unfortunately true, and not just because of my looks. His apartment was peppered with yellow Post-its reminding him of the names of things: "thermostat," "smoke detector," "VCR—insert tape before recording," "milk—check date—month day AND year."

He showed me a cruddy garbage bag in his closet. I've saved every one since 1983, he said.

I let it go.

Hook, Line and Sinker
Judy Budnitz

Short Story
F, 30s
Contemporary
Comic

If you've ever had sex in a fishing boat, raise your hand. If you're never going to have sex in a fishing boat after reading this, raise your hand.

I was dating a fisherman. I like to go out with him in his boat early in the morning when he hauled in the nets. (. . .)

He had a hammer that he used sometimes to bonk them on the head if they flopped around too much. He liked to stick his fingers in the slits of their gills as they breathed their last breaths. They can't even feel it, it's just reflex, he'd say as juicy fish-flesh pulsed around his fingers, squeezing and fluttering.

He had an erection tenting his raincoat. I pretended I didn't see, but I wanted to bonk it on the head with his hammer.

Sometimes the fisherman couldn't even wait to get back to the docks; he had to start slitting them open right there on the boat. (. . .) He would have me lie down on the slippery piles of fish, scales and fins pricking right through my clothes, all those wide-open eyes pressing into the back of my neck. (. . .)

You have such a beautiful body, he would say at these times, you do.

Which is always a lie, I know, it is something people say when they want something from you. (. . .)

Sometimes when we were making love he missed my body entirely and plunged himself deep into the pile of fish. He always pretended it was an accident.

Hook, Line and Sinker

Judy Budnitz

Short Story
F, 30s
Contemporary
Comic

Dating nightmare #474.

I brought the deaf man to Sunday dinner with my family.

Are you sure he's deaf? He doesn't look deaf, my mother said.

His ears look just fine to me, said my father. (. . .)

Can he read lips? My sister asked and mouthed: Eat me. (. . .)

Does he have one of those dogs? You know I'm allergic to dogs, my father said.

My god, Harold. He's deaf not blind, my mother hissed. (. . .)

By this point my sister was in his lap.

Well he certainly seems friendly, my mother said brightly. He seems to like people.

And he's even house-trained, my father said sarcastically. Stop talking about him like he's a pet.

Sheldon was running his fingertips over my sister, he was reading her like Braille, he was skipping straight to the good parts. (. . .)

He must be French, isn't he? Or Italian? You know how Italians are. They kiss everybody. Twice.

No mother, I said and stood up to leave. (. . .)

He's just compensating, my mother said, you know, with his other senses, to make up for his hearing. I've read they do that. You know, like seeing, smelling . . . what else?

Touching, I said. (. . .) Sheldon, come, I called.

He didn't hear me.

Humoresque

Fannie Hurst

Short Story
F, 50s
Classical
Dramatic

*1919. A Russian Jewish mother is distraught because
her son, an accomplished violinist, has joined the
armed forces. On his last day at home, she loses it.*

I can't stand it! Can't! Can't! Take my life—take my
blood, but don't take my boy—don't take my boy! I can't
help it—can't! Cut out my heart from me, but let me keep
my boy—my wonder boy. (. . .) I can't help it, Leon; I'm
not one of those fine mothers that can be so brave. Cut
out my heart, but leave my boy! My wonder-boy—my
child I prayed for! A genius like you could so easy get ex-
cused, Leon. Give it up. Genius it should be the last to be
sent to—the slaughter-pen. Leon darlink—don't go! (. . .)

You should wait for the draft. With my Roody and
even my baby Boris enlisted, ain't it enough for one
mother? Since they got to be in camp, all right, I say, let
them be there, if my heart breaks for it, but not my
wonder-child! You can get exemption, Leon, right away
for the asking. Stay with me, Leon! Don't go away! The
people at home got to be kept happy with music. That's
being a soldier, too, playing their trouble away. Stay with
me, Leon! Don't go leave me—don't—don't—

In Which I Use the "F" Word More Times Than Is Probably Legal in Many States

Miss Doxie

Blog Entry
F, 25+
Contemporary
Comic

You try to take in a little culture, and what does it get you?

Last night Dukay took me out for a romantic evening, which was very nice of him, and which he planned all by himself. And the plan was to take me to the symphony, where we would listen to pretty instruments playing Christmas songs, and hold hands and be generally over-taken by the magic of Christmas as presented through "triangle" and "tuba." That was the plan.

But the plan did not work out so much, in the sense that we didn't actually do that, in the sense that we never quite made it inside, in the sense that PEOPLE, WE GOT KICKED OUT OF THE SYMPHONY.

Yes. I don't want to talk about it.

But I will say that the people at the symphony are RE-ALLY NOT KIDDING about shutting those doors at EX-ACTLY THE RIGHT TIME, even if that means allowing the people in line DIRECTLY in front of you inside and then abruptly pushing you OUT OF THE DOOR and INTO THE HALLWAY and then LOCKING THE DOOR IN YOUR FACE, while you stand there, amazed, because, HI. YOU JUST PUSHED ME OUT THE DOOR.

I don't think I have mentioned that the woman who pushed me out the door? HAD A RAT TAIL. She was like, sixty years old, and she had a rat tail. Because nothing says "high culture" like a rat tail! Nothing says "I have every right to be a snobby bitch to you, by the powers vested in me by my RAT TAIL," like a rat tail! Y'all, I could not make this shit up if I tried.

And I will also say that Dukay was not HAPPY about this turn of events. No. You can maybe imagine.

Jesus My Bantu Butt

Barbara Lindsay

Short Story
F, 30s
Contemporary
Seriocomic

*Tina Turner Washington is rootless, unemployed,
unapologetically sexual, and secretly desperate to
find her way to a cleaner, calmer way of living. In
church, she hopes to find comfort and guidance,
but her conversation with one of the church
matrons goes very wrong.*

Hell, bitch, that's not a very Jesusy thing to say. You
think you better'n me just 'cause you got a car and shit
and your nails is all done up like a hooker for God? No,
worse than that. You God's pimp. That's what you are.
You got on that hat and those red nails and that skirt and
shit, and you say it's so you can bring people to the Lord,
but then you say those shitty things to me about I'm
going to Hell if I don't believe what you say. What proof
I got that you know God? This guy you talkin' 'bout, he
sound like a real tight-assed son of a bitch to me, always
waitin' for you mess up so he can squash you like a bug. I
need that shit, I'll go on home to my daddy. This God
you pimpin' for, he don't sound like somebody I want
messin' with my holy soul. You think you so hot. How
come you get to be holy and nobody else is? Bring me to
the Lord, my Bantu butt. You ain't bringin' nobody to
nothin'. Only thing you make me wanna do is take a
shower, wash your scowlin' God offa me.

Jubilation, Florida

N. M. Kelly

Short Story
F, 40+
Contemporary
Comic

Two married, middle-aged consenting adults pre-pare for a sexual tryst. First things first, however.

Two things before we go any further. (. . .) First, my husband is the kindest, most gentle man I have ever met. I clearly don't deserve him. He's like a surfing, golfing St. Francis of Assisi. If he ever finds out he may want to kill you, but he's so kind-hearted, and not very well organized, so he couldn't pull it off. I'd have to do it. I'm kind of his "go-to" guy. Just thought you should know. (. . .) Afterwards, I'm planning to burn your body and sprinkle your ashes on my roses. (. . .) Bone marrow is a superior fertilizer, plus I've kind of gotten used to you hanging around—so, it would be the best of both worlds. Well, for me of course. You'd be mulch. (. . .)

Maybe we can stop talking now.

Les Miserables

Victor Hugo, Translator Isabel F. Hapgood

Novel
F, 20s-30s
Classical
Dramatic

Fantine, having resorted to prostitution, pleads with police inspector Javert.

Monsieur Javert, I beseech your mercy. I assure you that I was not in the wrong. (. . .) I swear to you by the good God that I was not to blame! That gentleman, the bourgeois, whom I do not know, put snow in my back. Has any one the right to put snow down our backs when we are walking along peaceably, and doing no harm to anyone? I am rather ill, as you see. (. . .) Monsieur Javert, good Monsieur Inspector! is there not some person here who saw it and can tell you that this is quite true? Perhaps I did wrong to get angry. (. . .) Don't put me in prison! You see, there is a little girl who will be turned out into the street to get along as best she may, in the very heart of the winter; and you must have pity on such a being, my good Monsieur Javert. If she were older, she might earn her living; but it cannot be done at that age. I am not a bad woman at bottom. It is not cowardliness and gluttony that have made me what I am. If I have drunk brandy, it was out of misery. (. . .) When I was happy, it was only necessary to glance into my closets, and it would have been evident that I was not a coquettish and untidy woman. (. . .) Have pity on me, Monsieur Javert!

Losing a Glass Slipper

Emily Brauer Rogers

Poem
F, Teen+
Contemporary
Seriocomic

*While reading a bedtime fairy tale, the narrator
pauses to tell the "real" story.*

Cinderella's shoes really were too tight.

Not tight as in "hack off your toes or heel like the step-
  sisters longing for a prince" tight. Rather they were
  the tight "that makes you wince when you put them
  on,
but after five minutes your foot is numb
so you forget about it until you take off your shoe and
notice the two blisters gently oozing blood after a night of
  dancing" tight.

Godmothers aren't fail-proof.
And Cinderella didn't say "Excuse me, Godmother, these
  are a little snug."
She was supposed to wear the shoes, snug or not, so she
  wore the shoes.
Cinderella was a good girl.
The story goes.

Cinderella would have loved to go to the ball barefoot.
The cold smooth marble

on the balls of her feet.
When she lost that shoe, God, how good it felt.
That one foot against the grass among the evening dew,
in the puddles where the mud squished and caked around
her toes.

The Mission of Jane
Edith Wharton

Short Story
F, 20s
Classical
Dramatic

1904. Mrs. Lethbury has fallen in love with an infant named Jane, and knowing her husband will be reluctant to adopt, tentatively makes her case.

I want—I have wanted so dreadfully . . . it has been such a disappointment . . . not to . . .

It wasn't your fault. I never told you—but when I chose that rose-bud paper for the front-room upstairs, I always thought—it would be such a pretty paper—for a baby—to wake up in. That was years ago, of course; but it was rather an expensive paper . . . and it hasn't faded in the least . . . and so I thought . . . as we don't use the room for anything . . . now that Aunt Sophronia is dead . . . I thought I might . . . you might . . . oh, Julian, if you could only have seen it just waking up in its crib!

I'm so lonely without a little child—and I thought perhaps you'd let me adopt one . . . It's at the hospital . . . its mother is dead . . . and I could . . . pet it, and dress it, and do things for it . . . and it's such a good baby . . . you can ask any of the nurses . . . it would never, never bother you by crying . . . the nurse is *sure* she must be a lady's child.

Momster

Irene Ziegler

Short Story
F, 45-50
Contemporary
Comic

A mother is jealous of her young son's girlfriend.

My fourteen-year-old son, Jesse, is in love. Amanda, at the tender age of sixteen, is an oversexed, tail-waggling, boy-eating harlot from Hell.

I complain to my neighbor, Jill. "She has her own room, her own car, her own cell phone, her own cell phone *number—.*"

"Well, there's not much point to having your own cell phone without your own number," Jill says. Jill has an unfortunate overbite, which prevents her from being pretty.

"My *point* is that Amanda has been raised with no limits. And not only that," I say, "She is obviously sexually experienced, and I don't want my son around someone like that."

"You're sexually experienced," Jill says. "And he's around you all the time."

The remark has an unfortunate effect on my urinary sphincter. I retreat before giving Jill the moral upper hand.

Alone with my daytime wine, I brood. Because of Amanda, Jesse has a sudden predilection for boxer shorts and MTV. He takes long showers twice a day, and calls me *Momster*, which, as you can hear, is only one letter away from *Monster*, and I can just hear them together, alone in the dark, making fun of my age spots and receding gums. Momster, indeed.

It can't go on. It won't. Amanda must die.

Momster

Irene Ziegler

Short Story
F, 50s
Contemporary
Seriocomic

*When her son complains about her drinking, a
lonely mom considers rehab.*

I want very few things from life: my children, a sleeveless
dress that hides the ugly part under my arm, a good diet
wine. I'm thinking now I should add rehab to the list. If
nothing else, I might shed a few pounds. I almost signed
up when I heard Mel Gibson was at Wonderland Center,
but I was afraid I'd get stuck in equine therapy with Paris
Hilton and have NOTHING to say. And I'm an interesting person. Brittany Spears could learn from me. "Stop
having babies," I'd tell her. "They grow up, then leave
you!" To Lindsay Lohan: "I understand your self-
destructiveness; if I were you, I'd want to hurt me, too."
We'd form a bond, Lindsay and me, share spa cuisines,
massages, skin-care tips. We'd stay up late, talking, in
our designer bungalow. Under no circumstances would
we allow the Iraqi war to intrude, mostly because Lindsay
isn't conversant on the subject. Oh, what a rich escape I
imagined! I wonder what stopped me. Was it the thought

of David Hasselhoff eating food off the floor? Maybe it was the sixty grand for the month-long stay. Maybe it was the danger of catching a glimpse of myself in a mirror.

Most Memorable Character

Jacqueline T. Lynch

Short Story
F, 20s
Contemporary
Seriocomic

A young woman recalls being aided by a most surprising Samaritan.

That scary, nasty girl muttered an obscenity and flicked her cigarette away, hollered for someone to get a teacher. Nobody moved until she grabbed a kid and told him she would kill him on the spot if he didn't get his ass in that building and bring back a teacher in ten seconds. He got the teacher. I realize it was really for his own preservation and not mine, but I still appreciate it.

She sat down on the blacktop and lifted my head and shoulders into her lap to keep me from slamming my head on the ground. She stuck her dirty fingers down my throat and kept my airway open, to a background chorus of "Eewww!"

She told them what they could do to themselves.

When I lost bladder control, she covered me with her jean jacket. The school nurse, the vice principal, and pretty soon, the ambulance found us this way, the most composed two people in the chaotic school yard, me because I was totally unconscious by this time as the seizure had passed, and the school-yard thug, because she was utterly fearless.

She is my most memorable person.

My Son

Rita Stallard

Short Story
F, 50+
Contemporary
Dramatic

*An Australian grandmother comforts a young girl
sent to bed without dinner.*

Sh sh sh, Gran's here. C'mon lass, hush. Hush now. Stop
that nonsense. Here wipe those tears. Sit yourself up; I've
brought some tea. Shush, there'll be none of that. Now
where's my brave girlie? We'll be having none of the blub-
ber, or like as not he'll be in to see what all the fuss is
about, then we'll both be in bother. There's a good girl,
now eat your bread.

You're a big girl now, and you've to learn not to rile
him. Shush, be still and eat up. I'll not be listening to any
of it. Neither here nor there, whose was the doing. You've
to learn to mind your manners. He's your father and
that's an end to it. Hurry up now and be done.

I've some ointment for the strap. No one will know.
There'll be nought to see. There now. You snuggle down
and I'll tuck you in. All be forgotten tomorrow.

Sleep tight lass. I'll be in, in a bit.

He's a good man, really . . . my son.

Neighborhood Watch

Wendi Aarons

Blog Entry
F, 30+
Contemporary
Comic

*In suburbia, drama is scarce. So what's a suburban
mother to do?*

My annoying neighbors are moving. Heading off to parts
unknown. Slippin'-out-the-back Jack and makin'-a-new-
plan, Stan. And as I watch them pack up their sticky be-
longings, I can't wait for them to leave. But I sure will
miss them.

They sold their house in a mere two weeks, advertising it as a "Tuscan Delight!" Of course, the closest that
house has ever come to resembling an Italian villa was
probably when the twelve-year-old genius living there
smeared pizza on the wall, but I guess it wouldn't have
sold as quickly being touted as a "Cat-Piss Charmer!" or
a "Weedy Wonderland!" Those realtors know what
they're doing.

When we moved next door to these people two years
ago, I eagerly waited for them to welcome us to the
neighborhood. I'm still waiting. Sure, I could have gone
over there and introduced myself, but doesn't etiquette
say they should make the first move? Besides, then I
couldn't have launched my one-sided grudge match
against them. When the suburbs don't offer enough
drama, offer some of your own, baby.

Now, I *know* you remember so and so

Doris Davenport

Poem
F, 25+
Contemporary
Seriocomic

*We are our stories—and the manner in which
we tell them . . .*

["Now, I *know* you remember so and so . . . "]
meaning somebody who rode through town once, ten
years ago or who lived and died before your birth. They
expect you to remember, to know, just like your mind is
their mind and if you don't, they might take it personal.
Get so mad at you, they can't get on with the story.

Not like Fannie Mae. She will get all into a story and
catch herself: "But that was before *you*
were born." Fannie Mae will pause, grin for emphasis
and say, "And I *wish* you
coulda seen it!"

not me.
when i get through
when i'm done
won't be no *wishing*
you could see.
you gone   *see.*

Only Skin Deep
Kimberly Lester

Short Story
Female, 60s
Contemporary
Comic

*Judy Sinclair, a plastic surgery junkie, talks to a
woman in the doctor's waiting room.*

First time? I could tell. I haven't seen a nose with a hump
like that in years. A rhinoplasty should do you some
good. You also might want to consider Botox. You're
going to love Dr. Caldwell. He's done wonders for me.
Guess my age. Come on, don't be shy, guess. Just guess.

That's the oldest I've gotten. Usually people are afraid
to say anything above forty. But you know what? I'm
turning sixty next month. After Dr. Caldwell is through
with you, I'll bet you'll look thirty again. You are? I
thought you were at least thirty-five.

Anyway, I'm here for my check-up. Can you guess
what I've had done? I know it might be hard, but I'll
stand up to give you a hint. Notice anything unusually
fabulous for my age. Let me give you the full 360 degrees.
Here I'll even do a little wiggle. That's right, I've had ass
implants! Here, Honey, feel how natural they are. Go
ahead, Honey, it's just an ass. Oh, don't just poke at it.
Grab the whole thing, like this. Isn't this the best ass
you've ever felt?

Well, nice talking to you. Remember—two words—
BO TOX.

The Other Side of Air

Jeanne Braselton

Novel
F, 36
Contemporary
Dramatic

Anne's husband, Wyatt, has given her an un-wrapped, anonymous-feeling birthday present, saying he hadn't tried harder because she was so difficult to please. Now, Anne packs a suitcase.

I saw a thoughtless birthday present coming, Wyatt, and now I'm seeing me in Florida with my parents, and you shut up in that little house with your father, no wife, no baby, and nothing to take the edge off the misery. Think about that while I'm at the hotel, enjoying a private birthday present. And as for not being able to satisfy me with a birthday present, Wyatt, that's bullshit. (. . .) I would have been thrilled with a box of toothpicks if it came with some indication you love me. (. . .) You can bet your father never treated your mother like you do me, Wyatt.

I'm thirty-six years old, Wyatt. I'm too old to beg for affection. I'm too old to consider moving to the other side of the country with a man who won't even hold my hand on the way there. (. . .) As close to death as your mother's been, Wyatt, I wish I could trade places with her long enough for your father to look at me the way he looks at her. Remember his eyes the last time we saw him? They had everything in them. You call me difficult to please, but how hard would it be to give the gift of looking at me in such a loving way?

P.O.U.G.H.K.E.E.P.S.I.E.

Bara Swain

Short Short Story
F, 20+
Contemporary
Seriocomic

A young Southern woman longs for a normal life.

My daddy says that *average* is just a seven-letter word between *automatic transmission* and *avocado*. But the truth
of the matter is—I'm not very smart. That's why Mama
says to dress in bright clothes—to kinda throw everybody
off track. I tell all my male acquaintances that I was
kicked in the head by a two-hundred-and-fifty-pound
porker. Unless the male in question is also a two-hundred-
and-fifty-pound porker, then I tell him it was a wild
horse.

My cousin Billy, who's dyslexic and divorced twice,
told me I was titillating in 1988. T.I.T.I.L.L.A.T.I.N.G. I
can spell Poughkeepsie, New York, too, but I like titillating better. It's got such a nice ring to it!

I let cousin Billy sweet-talk me into an uncompromis-
ing position that I was sure he couldn't—you know—
complete, being a man of his affliction. I came this close
to becoming cousin Billy's third wife except that I wanted
children more than anything else in the world, even more
than cousin Billy. And actually, I still do. Want children, I
mean. More than anything.

My daddy says that *baby* is just a four-letter word between *baboon* and *Bazooka Joe*. Now, I may not be
smart, but I think my daddy is full of . . . of . . .
F.E.E.S.I.E.S.

Pack Job

Laura Jacqmin

Short Story
F, 15-19
Contemporary
Seriocomic

Lydia's scientist mother has recently moved to Antarctica. Lydia's younger brother, Joe, tells her she is old enough to move out and move on—but she isn't so sure.

I need to find a suitcase. Joe doesn't seem to understand that I can't leave unless I have a bag to put things in.

I don't want much.

A shirt, some pants. Extra socks.

I would like to take some rings.

A few pieces of glass, and magnets.

Cough syrup.

A ball of yarn.

I remember Mother reading a book to me when I was little, about a dog who had everything in the entire world that mattered. A thermometer, two feathered pillows.

Eye drops, ear drops, bottles of pills. A brass bell with her name on it.

All in a black leather bag with gold buckles. She had everything but experience.

And then a lion ate her bag with shiny buckles, so she had nothing.

I don't even have a bag. If I did, I would put all my

experience inside and close the buckles with a "snap!"
and feed it to a lion.

But still, I have no bag,

So.

I'll put everything I need in my pockets, or my hands.

And I'll just walk away.

And I'll do it *soon*.

Soon.

I swear.

The Possessed

Fydor Dostoevsky, Translator Constance Garnett

Novel
F, 40+
Classical
Seriocomic

Varvara Stavrogin makes a less-than-compelling case to young Dasha for marrying the fifty-three-year-old Stepan.

Stay, hold your tongue, don't be in a hurry! You're a sensible girl, and there must be no mistakes in your life. Now . . . though you will have money under my will, yet when I die, what will become of you, even if you have money? You'll be deceived and robbed of your money, you'll be lost in fact. But married to him you're the wife of a distinguished man. (. . .) Stay, I've not finished. He's frivolous, shilly-shally, cruel, egoistic, he has low habits. But mind you think highly of him, in the first place because there are many worse. (. . .) He's an old woman, but you know, that's all the better for you. You understand me, don't you? Do you understand me? He will complain of you, he'll begin to say things against you behind your back, he'll whisper things against you to any stray person he meets, he'll be forever whining and whining; (. . .) but he won't be able to get on without you all the same, and that's the chief thing. Make him obey you. (. . .) He'll want to hang himself, and threaten to—don't you believe it. It's nothing but nonsense. (. . .)

Come, you consent, eh? Will you say something at last?

The Princess Bride

William Goldman

Novel
F, 17
Contemporary
Comic

Buttercup kind of likes Westley.

I love you, I know this must come as something of a surprise, since all I've ever done is scorn you and degrade you and taunt you, but I have loved you for several hours now, and every second, more. I thought an hour ago that I loved you more than any woman has ever loved a man, but a half hour after that I knew that what I felt before was nothing compared to what I felt then. But ten minutes after that, I understood that my previous love was a puddle compared to the high seas before a storm. Your eyes are like that, did you know? Well they are. How many minutes ago was I? Twenty? Had I brought my feelings up to then? It doesn't matter. I love you so much more now than twenty minutes ago that there cannot be comparison.

The Princess Bride
William Goldman

Novel
F, 17
Contemporary
Comic

Buttercup wants Westley.

There is no room in my body for anything but you. My arms love you, my ears adore you, my knees shake with blind affection. My mind begs you to ask it something so it can obey. Do you want me to follow you for the rest of your days? I will do that. Do you want me to crawl? I will crawl. I will be quiet for you or sing for you, or if you are hungry, let me bring you food, or if you have thirst and nothing will quench it but Arabian wine, I will go to Araby, even though it is across the world, and bring a bottle back for your lunch. Anything there is that I can do for you, I will do for you; anything there is that I cannot do, I will learn to do. I know I cannot compete with the Countess in skills or wisdom or appeal, and I saw the way she looked at you. And I saw the way you looked at her. But remember, please, that she is old and has other interests, while I am seventeen and for me there is only you. Dearest Westley—I've never called you that before, have I?—Westley, Westley, Westley, Westley, Westley,—darling Westley, adored Westley, sweet perfect Westley, whisper that I have a chance to win your love.

The Queen of Chiva

Robert Crisman

Novella
F, 22
Contemporary
Seriocomic

*"Chiva" is West Coast street lingo for heroin.
Michelle, a junkie, has just quit treatment in
favor of ripping and running with her good
buddy, Roanne.*

God, Roanne! They put me out on the ward with all the
other assholes and—*fuck*, Roanne, I swear. And *then*,
guess who I run into right off the bat? Chili, the old
twelve-step guru of gurus himself.

He's a counselor there, right, and I've been there like
five minutes or something, and he's, "Oh, Michelle, so
good to *see* you, ready to get clean now?" Yuk yuk yuk,
like it's a big fucking joke. I just wanted to spit on him,
man. And, like I'm his project now, right? So he's always
cornering me, "What are you gonna do now, Michelle?
You need to get back to meetings, Michelle. Really,
Michelle. Us addicts, we're blah blah blah blah." Shit.

And *then*, they bring in these Ozzie and Harriet
motherfuckers from all over, right, and they're *sharing*,
you know, and just, tra la-la la-la, their higher power
took them out to lunch last Tuesday and picked up the
tab, and gee, isn't recovery just *wonderful*, and—I swear

to *God*, Roanne, just *listening* to those people'd give you a bad case of sugar diabetes.

So anyway, by last night I'd had it, you know, so I just said fuck it and called you, and here I am. Let's go have an adventure or something.

The Queen of Harlem
Brian Keith Jackson

Short Story
F, 45+
Contemporary
Comic

*An African-American real estate agent, dressed in
expensive clothes, unknowingly shows a client the
gentrified Harlem house he grew up in.*

Mr. Randolph? (. . .)

Diane Turner. (. . .) So nice to meet you. Sorry I'm
tardy, but this area is booming, and I've had to show four
other town houses today. Of course, this one is the prize.
(. . .)

Just listen. You hear that? That's the sound of history.

(. . .) Harlem is definitely the place to be. It's as the
kids say, "All that." You'll find this town house to be a
worthy investment. The best space for the buck. It's all in
the details.

(. . .) I don't normally advertise, but I used to be the
only broker handling properties up here. White brokers
wouldn't touch it with a gloved hand when it was just
shit. Anyone can appreciate the harvest, but few have
seen the seeds I've sown. We do what we can. I'm sure as
a young brother, and a lawyer no less, you understand. (. . .)
Did you say you were married? (. . .)

Well, FYI, a great many gay people have moved into
the neighborhood. Follow the gays, I say. They really are

the best people. Just fabulous. Give gays a ghetto, and they'll fix it right up . . . Not that I'm implying you're gay, but if you were, just know, it certainly wouldn't be held against you.

A Racial Education, Part Two

Gerald Early

Essay
F, teen
Contemporary
Dramatic

The author's daughter comes home from school one day, and slams the door.

The black kids at school are stupid (. . .).

Do you know what they said to me today? They said I must be biracial, that one of my parents must be white. (. . .)

They say I sound like a white person, so one of my parents must be white. They're so stupid. What am I supposed to do? Talk like them? Go around cursing all the time or saying "y'all" and "ain't" and stuff like that? Is that supposed to be the way black people talk? I know you and Mommy and your black friends, and the black people at church, and none of you guys talk like that. What am I supposed to sound like, a rap record? I don't like being called white. I'm not white and I'm not biracial. I think they're just ignorant.

A Racial Education, Part Two

Gerald Early

Essay
F, teen
Contemporary
Dramatic

The author's daughter galvanizes her identity.

No, I don't like that stuff that the black kids wear (. . .).
They're these Africa-crazy kids and they hate me.
They go around wearing these Mother Africa shirts and
stuff like that. They call me and Ros Oreos and everything. But in history class they couldn't even name any
countries in Africa when the teacher asked. I was naming
bunches and bunches of countries from the stuff I read
here at home. But they didn't know anything, yet they
want to think they're so black. I don't want anything to
do with them or wear anything they wear. I'm black and
I'm not ashamed of it. And I don't need a shirt to tell
anybody I'm black or to tell anybody I'm not ashamed.
All I have to do is live my life the way I want to.

Random Spam

Anonymous

Found Text
M/F, 20+
Contemporary
Comic

From a random, spam e-mail promoting under-valued stock, this text struck us as bizarrely performable. Maybe.

The Scooby snack teaches the tornado. Any lover can share a shower with the cloud formation inside the tomato, but it takes a real recliner to bury the moldy globule. A tape recorder seeks a sandwich. When you see the ski lodge, it means that the tattered customer goes to sleep. The underhandedly fractured mortician secretly plans an escape from a near industrial complex, and the plaintiff from the cashier makes love to a carelessly nuclear tape recorder.

Now and then, a briar patch goes deep sea fishing with a nation from a rattlesnake. Any oil filter can compete with some scythe, but it takes a real pit viper to ridiculously bestow great honor upon a mastodon. When a nuclear customer is paternal, the flatulent avocado pit lazily recognizes a vaporized cowboy. Most people believe that some turkey single-handedly secretly admires a mortician, but they need to remember how single-handedly a self-actualized avocado pit returns home.

Rappacini's Daughter
Nathaniel Hawthorne

Short Story
F, late teens
Classical
Dramatic

Beatrice's father, a mad botanical scientist, has imbued her with deadly powers, which her would-be lover, Giovanni, believes she intended to use against him.

Giovanni, why dost thou join thyself with me thus in those terrible words? I, it is true, am the horrible thing thou namest me. But thou,—what hast thou to do, save with one other shudder at my hideous misery to go forth out of the garden and mingle with thy race and forget that there ever crawled on Earth such a monster as poor Beatrice? (. . .)

I only dreamed to love thee a little time, and so to let thee pass away, leaving but thin image in mine heart; for Giovanni, believe it, though my body be nourished with poison, my spirit is God's creature, and craves love as its daily food. But my father,—he has united us in this fearful sympathy. Yes; spurn me, tread upon me, *kill* me! Oh what is death after such words as thine? But it was not I. Not for a world of bliss would I have done it.

Rubyfruit Jungle

Rita Mae Brown

Novel
F, 60+
Contemporary
Seriocomic

Carrie reconciles with her adult filmmaker daughter.

Well, I said all I got to say. I packed you sandwiches and
there's some Switzer cheese in wax paper. Buy yourself
some milk and have a good lunch. There's three hard-
boiled eggs, too, so you don't have to buy any food.
That's all your old mother can give you. (. . .)

I done the best I could. Honey, I'm so sorry I ain't
rich. I'd buy you a movie house of your own if I was. I
don't say nothing this week but it hurts me to see you so
drawn. You're too skinny, girl. You're up there working
and working yourself. You always was a hard worker. I'm
afraid you drive yourself too hard. Dammit to hell. I
grow up with nothing, and I want my kid to have something. You're starting out from scratch cause I got nothing to give you. I did the best I could. Don't hate me,
honey, don't hate me. (. . .)

And I never said that thing you said I said. I never
said you weren't mine. You are mine. (. . .)

I love you. You're the only thing I keep living for.
What else I got—the TV.

Run Away
J. Boyer

Short Story
F, 20s-30s
Contemporary
Comic

*While shopping in a mall, a mother tries to regain
control of her daughter—and herself.*

I know this is hard for you to understand, but Mommy
has a Masters Degree. She wrote her thesis on String
Theory and made a groundbreaking case that particles
of light change in direct proportion to the mass of the
waterline at the edge of a pond. Now Mommy can't tell
you where she put her glasses. Do you see? There is simply not enough of Mommy to go around sometimes.
She's like particles of light reflecting off the water.

That is why sometimes Mommy has to go into the
bathroom and say her name aloud twenty-five times, just
to be certain she actually exists.

Mommy is going to take a deep breath. See? Would
you like to take a deep breath too? That's it, honey. Now,
Mommy did not call you an asshole when you ignored
her.

That would be a sign Mommy's coming apart. Which
she's not. She's totally not. She would if she could, but
she can't. And you know why? Because Mommy has a
Master's Degree.

Samantha Paulson, 32; Milpitas, California

Eric Feezell

Essay
F, 32
Contemporary
Comic

Samantha Paulson's "anticlimactic" retelling of a near-death experience.

As I lay bleeding to death with a crushed skull and broken spine, pressed cruelly within the mangled frame of what used to be my Volkswagen Passat, my head began to swim and my body to feel light as a feather. By this time the pain had subsided, giving way to a euphoric feeling, something almost otherworldly. All I could see was this *light*, and I was like, "This is it, I am going to die. I am going to the other side now." I could have sworn I saw an angel in the distance, beckoning me forth, assuring me it would be OK. *Let go*, it whispered airily. *Let go*.

Well, the angel turned out to be a 220-pound unshaven paramedic with a flashlight screaming at me to unclench my hands from the steering wheel so they could extricate my contorted body from the wreckage, which apparently was about to explode. Go figure. Excessive blood loss and cranial trauma can really muddle your cognitive abilities, I guess.

Sexing the Cherry

Jeanette Winterson

Novel
F, 30+
Contemporary
Dramatic

*The Dog-Woman—a mythic, grotesque giant—
reflects on the birthing and naming of her son,
Jordan, a traveler of sorts.*

I had a name but I have forgotten it. They call me the
Dog-Woman and it will do. I call him Jordan and it will
do. He has no other name before or after. What was there
to call him, fished as he was from the stinking Thames? A
child can't be called Thames, no and not Nile either, for
all his likeness to Moses. But I wanted to give him a river
name, a name not bound to anything, just as the waters
aren't bound to anything. When a woman gives birth her
waters break and she pours out the child and the child
runs free. I would have liked to pour out a child from my
body but you have to have a man for that and there's no
man who's a match for me.

When Jordan was a baby he sat up on top of me as
much as a fly rests on a hill of dung. And I nourished him
as a hill of dung nourishes a fly, and when he had eaten
his fill he left me.

Jordan . . .

I should have named him after a stagnant pond and
then I could have kept him, but I named him after a river
and in the flood-tide he slipped away.

Sixteen at the Jeu De Paume

Maureen Ryan Griffin

Poem
F, 16
Contemporary
Dramatic

While touring Europe, a young woman visits the Jeu de Paume in Paris and is overcome by the Impressionist paintings surrounding her.

My God! I can't believe I'm here in Paris and just last
week I (Me!)
rode on the top of a double-decker bus in London so of
course
I was singing (sort of softly) . . . *I refused to ride*
on all those double-decker buses
all because there was no driver on the top
and last night the Eiffel Tower!
And walking to the Musée Jeu de Paume (doesn't it sound
better in French?)
after escaping the Louvre—all those religious paintings,
of course I snuck out
past Venus de Milo, or was it the Winged Victory?—
I saw French boys sailing boats
just like the picture in my French book back in Erie,
Pennsylvania
Oh bonjour, garcons! Comment allez-vous!
Hey, I can tell
if it's a Degas or a Renoir or a Seurat
God, I'm really good at art!

And even this guard staring as if he knows
I'd touch those strokes of magenta and umber and cerise
if I could
can't stop me from feeling
                    I belong here in Paris
Oh my God, to come upon
three panels of bliss with a bench in front
I could die right now!
drinking in *Water Lilies*
I know Monet painted just for me

The Speech of Polly Baker

Benjamin Franklin

Short Story
F, 30s
Classical
Seriocomic

1747. "The Speech of Miss Polly Baker before a Court of Judicature, at Connecticut near Boston in New England; where she was prosecuted the fifth time, for having a Bastard Child: Which influenced the Court to dispense with her Punishment, and which induced one of her Judges to marry her the next Day—by whom she had fifteen Children."

May it please the honourable bench to indulge me in a few words: This is the fifth time, gentlemen, that I have been dragg'd before your court on the same account; (. . .) Abstracted from the law, I cannot conceive (may it please your honors) what the nature of my offense is. I have brought five fine children into the world, at the risque of my life; Can it be a crime to add to the king's subjects, in a new country, that really wants people? I have debauched no other woman's husband, nor enticed any other youth; nor has any one the least cause of complaint against me, unless, perhaps the ministers of justice, because I have had children without being married, by which they have missed a wedding fee. But can this be a fault of mine? (. . .)

What must poor young women do, whom custom and nature forbid to solicit the men, and who cannot force themselves upon husbands, when the laws take no care to provide them any, and yet severely punish them if they do their duty without them; the duty of the first and great command of nature and nature's God, *encrease* [*sic*] *and multiply*; a duty, from the steady performance of which nothing has been able to deter me, but for its sake I have hazarded the loss of the publick esteem, and have frequently endured publick disgrace; and therefore ought, in my humble opinion, instead of a whipping, to have a statue erected to my memory.

Thank You, Thank You, Thank You

Zev Borow

Online Journal Blog
F, 42
Contemporary
Comic

*Hannah Karp, upon her recent engagement,
delivers a speech from the heart.*

I'm speechless. Thank goodness I prepared a few remarks
ahead of time. I have been dreaming about this moment
since I was a little girl, which, it's no secret, was a pretty
long time ago. So, yes, Mark, I accept your marriage pro-
posal! Even though I don't find you particularly attractive, or . . . I can't read this. Is good-smelling a word? I
can barely think. But thank you, Mark, you drive a
Lexus, and you bought me this ring, which is really
heavy! I can't believe I'm finally engaged! And to my
mother, who said it was wrong not to put my real photo
on that online dating site and that I would die alone. Go
to hell.

Thorazine Johnny Felsun Loves Me

Thom Jones

Short Story
F, teen
Contemporary
Dramatic

The narrator, a dreamy young woman, is given to melancholia. She just found out her cat died.

I used to kind of like people. That was before I was like a teenager and stuff. I got pinkeye in Nepal and my mother, who is a doctor an' all, paid no attention to me. My father is a psychiatrist. My parents don't give two shits about me. I was abused when I was little tho (sic) I can't remember all the details. (. . .)

I am so afraid sometimes. My life is boring but I have violent action-adventure nightmares and wake up more tired than when I went to bed. The days alone in my room are languorous empty centuries filled with dread and anguish. (. . .) I light up a Parliament on some nights and I look out into the night (. . .).

Sometimes on a clear night the firmament is filled with stars that are as beautiful as sapphires, diamonds, an all the jewels of the Earth multiplied to the twelfth power of infinity. At times like this I am filled with hope and know that in spite of my failures as a romantic novelist (. . .) people will fall at my feet and worship me. There will even be little bronze markers at the places I've been to, like Nepal where I suffered with pinkeye and complained not at all.

Thoughts of a Bride on Her Wedding Day

Janice Heffernan

Short Story
F, 20s
Contemporary
Comic

With her wedding moments away, a conflicted bride-to-be struggles.

I can't marry him. I'll be miserable. He'll be miserable. This dress makes me look ugly. My shoes are pinching my toes. His family hates me. I can't stand them, especially his sister. They all take advantage of him. I won't live my life with someone who takes care of his entire family all the time and hardly spends any time with me. Oh God, he wants six kids. I'll never survive giving birth to six kids. Is the priest naked underneath his robes? I can tell his legs are bare. I wonder what a priest looks like naked. I shouldn't be thinking these things. He loves me. I know he does. He tells me so over and over again but he treats me like I'm a child, someone who needs to be told what to do, why to do it and when to do it. I can't stand him. I don't love him. I care more for his best friend then I do for him. I have to tell him I can't marry him. Oh God, he's saying "I do." His eyes are incredible. He loves me. He just said so in front of everybody. I can't do this. Oh, I hate him for doing this to me. I love him, I have to say "I do." I don't want any other woman near him. He's mine forever and ever. No one can take him away from me.

to be a woman

Jennifer Karmin

Poem
F, 20
Contemporary
Seriocomic

*A young woman has mixed feelings about being
born female.*

to be a woman is to be a girl a girl a girl to wait to wait
talked over interrupted don't raise your hand you have a
penis and i have a vagina so you get to pee standing up
and i have to sit down a ten year old girl in love with an
eight year old redhead named julie herman who lives two
houses away who you kiss and touch and we have no
hair and her older brother found us naked and when we
grow up we want to be playboy centerfolds but the curse
i am a curse four girl cousins and then me and then my
brother the boy the little man when my brother was born
i said but where's the girl when i was born my grandfather martin came to the hospital drunk and said shame
it's not a boy and my grandma jean told him he should
leave or she was going to throw him out the window

The Tragedy of Pudd'nhead Wilson

Mark Twain

Novel
F, 30s
Classical
Dramatic

Mississippi, 1860s. Roxy, a slave, relives the moment she snapped and escaped.

'Bout ten days ago I 'uz sayin' to myself dat I couldn't las' many mo' weeks I 'uz so wore out wid de awful work en de lashin's, en so downhearted en misable. En I didn't care no mo', nuther—life warn't wuth noth'n' to me, if I got to go on like dat. Well, dey was a little sickly nigger girl 'bout ten year ole dat 'uz good to me, en hadn't no mammy, po' thing, en I loved her en she loved me; en she come out whah I 'uz workin' en she had a roasted tater, en tried to slip it to me—robbin' herself, you see, a'ca'se she knowed de overseer didn't give me enough to eat—en he ketched her at it, en give her a lick acrost de back wid his stick, which 'uz as thick as a broom handle, en she drop' screamin' on de groun', en squirmin' en wallerin' aroun' in de dust like a spider dat's got crippled. I couldn't stan' it. All de hellfire dat 'uz ever in my heart flame' up, en I snatch de stick outen his han' en laid him flat. He laid dah moanin' en cussin', en all out of his head, you know, en de niggers 'uz plumb sk'yred to death. Dey gathered roun' him to he'p him, en I jumped on his hoss en took out for de river as tight as I could go. I knowed what dey would do wid me.

The Tragedy of Pudd'nhead Wilson

Mark Twain

Novel
F, 30s
Classical
Dramatic

Mississippi, 1860s. Roxy, a slave on the run, tells Chambers the dangers faced in finding her way to him.

It 'uz gitt'n' towards dark. I 'uz at de river in two minutes. Den I see a canoe, en I says dey ain't no use to drown myself tell I got to; so I went on a-spinnin' down de river—paddled mo'n two days—and when I got here I went straight to whah you used to wuz, en den I come to dis house, en dey say you's away but 'spected back every day; so I didn't dast to go down de river to Dawson's, 'ca'se I might miss you. Well, las' Monday I 'uz pass'n by one o' dem places in fourth street whah deh sticks up runaway nigger bills, en he'ps to ketch 'em, en I seed my marster! I 'mos' flopped down on de groun', I felt so gone. He had his back to me, en 'uz talkin' to de man en givin' him some bills—nigger bills, I reckon, en I's de nigger. He's offerin' a reward—dat's it. Ain't I right, don't you reckon? *(Pause—apprehension in her voice.)* Turn up dat light! I want to see yo' face better. Dah now—lemme look at you. Chambers, you's as white as yo' shirt! Has you see dat man? Has he be'n to see you?

The Turn of the Screw

Henry James

Short Story
F, 20s-30s
Classical
Dramatic

*1898. From their secretive and precocious behavior,
the governess concludes the children in her charge
are being wooed to the dark side by two evil
ghosts. She reveals her suspicions to the house-
keeper, Mrs. Grose.*

The four, depend upon it, perpetually meet. The more I've
watched and waited the more I've felt that if there were
nothing else to make it sure it would be made so by the
systematic silence of each. *Never*, by a slip of the tongue,
have they so much as alluded to either of their old
friends, any more than Miles has alluded to his expulsion.
Oh yes, we may sit here and look at them, and they may
show off to us there to their fill: but even while they pre-
tend to be lost in their fairy-tale they're steeped in their
vision of the dead restored. He's not reading to her,
they're talking of *them*—they're talking horrors! I go on,
I know, as if I were crazy; and it's a wonder I'm not.
What I've seen would have made *you* so; but it has only
made me more lucid, made me get hold of still other
things. It's a game. Yes, mad as that seems! They haven't
been good—they've only been absent. It has been easy to
live with them, because they're simply leading a life of
their own. They're not mine—they're not ours. They're
his and they're hers! Quint's and that woman's! They
want to get to them. (. . .) They can destroy them!

The Undomestic Goddess
Sophie Kinsella

Novel
F, 29
Contemporary
Comic

*Workaholic attorney Samantha Sweeting can
barely spare the time to fill out the intake question-
naire for an "Ultimate De-Stress Experience" at the
Green Tree Center.*

Would you consider yourself stressed?
*No. I'm not stressed. I'm . . . busy. Plenty of people
are busy. I have a high-powered job, my career is important to me, and I enjoy it. OK. So sometimes I do feel a
bit tense. But I'm a lawyer in the City, for God's sake.
What do you expect?* My handwriting is pressing so hard
into the page, I've torn the paper. Dammit. Never mind.
Let's move on to the next question.

**On average, how many hours do you spend in the office
every day?**
~~14~~
~~12~~
~~8~~
It depends.

Do you exercise regularly?
~~I regularly go swimming~~
~~I occasionally go swim~~

I am intending to begin a regular regime of swimming.
When I have time. Work's been busy lately, it's a blip.

Do you drink 8 glasses of water a day?
~~Yes~~
~~Someti~~
No. (. . .)
(TO SPA ATTENDANT) I did mention that I'm in a
bit of a hurry (. . .). Are all these questions absolutely
necessary? (. . .)
I don't have time for this. I really do not have the
time.

Wants

Grace Paley

Short Story
F, 40+
Contemporary
Seriocomic

*A woman relates an encounter with her
ex-husband.*

I saw my ex-husband in the street. I was sitting on the
steps of the new library.

Hello, my life, I said. We had once been married for
twenty-seven years, so I felt justified.

He said, What? What life? No life of mine.

I said, O.K. I don't argue when there's real disagree-
ment. I got up and went into the library to see how much
I owed them.

The librarian said $32 even and you've owed it for
eighteen years. I didn't deny anything. Because I don't understand how time passes. I have had those books. I have
often thought of them. The library is only two blocks
away.

My ex-husband followed me to the Books Returned
desk. He interrupted the librarian, who had more to tell.
In many ways, he said, as I look back, I attribute the dis-
solution of our marriage to the fact that you never invited
the Bertrams to dinner.

That's possible, I said. But really, if you remember:
first, my father was sick that Friday, then the children
were born, then I had those Tuesday-night meetings, then

the war began. Then we didn't seem to know them any more. But you're right. I should have had them to dinner.

I gave the librarian a check for thirty-two dollars. Immediately she trusted me, put my past behind her, wiped the record clean.

The Way of the Woman Warrior

Kathleen Statham

Memoir
F, 30+
Contemporary
Seriocomic

A woman addresses her new therapist.

I dodged three bullets, Doctor; how could I not be fine? With just one breast, I can have a mammogram in half the time. I can be squeezed, literally, into the last five minutes before the lab tech's lunch hour. And since the mastectomy, my husband's made up new endearments for me, like "beloved unicorn." Cute, huh?

What else? Well, the hysterectomy after my cervical cancer wiped out my libido for awhile. (. . .) Lubricants to the rescue! Now our sex life is one slippery slide of a ride with Astroglide!

And forget about gastric bypass surgery for losing weight. Grow a malignant tumor, instead, like I did, and have half your stomach removed. It's a perfect way to shrink the body.

Yes, Doctor, I've been sliced, diced, and scooped out; stapled and stitched back together. All so I could come here and tell you about it.

My *feelings*? Uh, . . . You know what? I don't think so, not today. I want to hang onto *those* a little longer, thank you!

The Wedding

CC Thomas

Short Story
F, 20s
Contemporary
Dramatic

*A young bride-to-be informs her father of a tough
decision.*

. . . Yes, everything is going according to plan. Mom and
I have been hard at work tying down the last details and
that's really what I want to talk to you about today.
(*Takes a deep breath, apparently nervous.*) I'm trying to
turn this into the perfect wedding, if there is such a thing,
especially in our family. I want this to be a really tradi-
tional wedding, old-fashioned with horse and carriage
and the whole bit, but I just can't squeeze everybody into
the picture. There are just a few things that look wrong in
my mind when I try to visualize that final moment when
the music begins and I turn around to see that man who
walks me down the aisle. (*Pause*) I just don't see you
there. I've tried picturing it every way I could think of.
I even thought maybe you and Michael could do, you
know, one of either side like a couple of Dad-bookends.
But, Dad, it just doesn't feel right. I know you've been the
best dad that you could, but for so long Michael has been
my day-to-day father. You're my weekend dad and while
Michael could never take your place, (*Pause.*) you can't
take his either. I know that you love me more than anything else and I know that anything I ask you to do, if

you can, you will do it for me. Today, Daddy, I'm going to ask you *not* to walk me down the aisle at my wedding. I know you'll understand, Daddy, because I've understood all these years the place I had in your life, waiting patiently on the outskirts. I know you don't like it; but I know you'll do it because you love me even though you couldn't say it every day, the way that Michael can.

What the Pharmacist Said

Greg Machlin

Novel
F, 20s - early 30s
Contemporary
Seriocomic

The Diary of H is set in a fascist state. Various minor characters from Shakespeare's plays meet up in unexpected ways. The Pharmacist, recast from Romeo and Juliet, is angry, smart, and afraid. She smokes throughout.

. . . Two weeks ago, a customer wants a sleeping potion, to fake this chick's death. Highly illegal. But I made it for him 'cause he's a priest. Big mistake. But he thanks me, blesses me, leaves.

Three days later, front page of the NEW VERONA POST: "TRIPLE HOMICIDE IN CEMETERY! TRAGEDY STRIKES!" The religious guy's *quoted* in it, and—Jesus! The girl who drank my potion is *dead*.

Only I can't be upset 'cause of these *cameras*. If someone checks the tapes, there might be questions. I could lose my job . . . or worse.

You know what's twisted? When I found out my potion *worked*, and the chick didn't die from it—she offed herself some other way—I actually took some pride in my work before I remembered she & her boyfriend were dead.

But I'm still responsible! *I made the potion*. If I had said no to the priest, the girl would still be alive.

She'd be "unhappy"? So what? *Everybody's* unhappy! Do you know anyone who's happy? And if you do, can you point them out to me so I can *shoot* them for being so stupid?

Country like this, if you're happy, you're not paying attention and you don't deserve to live. They kill people for less, you know?

Who Am I This Time?

Kurt Vonnegut Jr.

Short Story
F, 20s-30s
Contemporary
Dramatic

Realizing that her audition for the part of Stella in A Streetcar Named Desire completely lacked passion, Helene breaks down before the director of the North Crawford Mask and Wig Club.

I was terrible, wasn't I? (. . .) I'm a walking icebox, and I know it. (. . .)

When people get to know me, that's what they say. (. . .) I don't want to be the way I am. (. . .) I just can't help it, living the way I've lived all my life. The only experiences I've had have been in crazy dreams of movie stars. When I meet somebody nice in real life, I feel as though I were in some kind of big bottle, as though I couldn't touch that person, no matter how hard I tried. (. . .)

You ask me if I've ever been in love. (. . .) No—but I want to be. I know what this play's about. I know what Stella's supposed to feel and why she feels it. I—I—I—(. . .) I just don't know how to begin.

Why Are You Laughing?

Tom Coash

Short Short Story
F, 25-35
Contemporary
Dramatic

Written for a spousal-abuse project.

"If you ever leave me, I'll kill you."

We were watching this late night talk show . . . "Has the romance gone out of your marriage?" Without thinking I laughed. "Why are you laughing?," said my husband George. Very controlled, my husband. Never a hair out of place, a wife out of line, or an emotion out of control. He never, for instance, hits me in public or where it will show.

"Why did you laugh?"

Clothes by Armani, hair by Horst, fractured ribs by George. At the hospital I broke down crying on the examination table. It was suggested that I meet with a psychiatrist. I took several tests and he said I scored high on the paranoia scale.

I asked what that meant.

"You have an irrational fear that someone is out to get you."

I think, sometimes, of those Chinese women with bound feet. I feel close to them. Bound by wrappings, social . . . economic . . . physical.

"Why did you laugh?" he asked. I said it was nothing. After a pause he said,

"If you ever leave me, I'll kill you."

And I believe him.

Why I Shouldn't Take Sudafed On an Empty Stomach

Wendi Aarons

Blog Entry
F, 30+
Contemporary
Comic

Hi, Mrs. Johnson. I'm here to pick up Sam from school.
Oh, I see the class had face painting today! That's great!
Wow—look at you, Mrs. Johnson! All painted up like a
tiger. And you're even wearing little tiger ears! I think
someone's husband is going to have themselves quite a
wild night tonight, ifyouknowwhatImean, girlfriend!
Grooowlll!

(*Long, uncomfortable silence.*)

Crap. Was that out loud?

(*Long, uncomfortable silence.*)

Guess this means I'll be chaperoning the field trip to
the waste treatment plant, huh?

(*Long, uncomfortable silence.*)

OK, well, see you tomorrow. BADASS TIGER LADY!

(*Long, uncomfortable silence.*)

That was out loud, too, wasn't it?

The Witch

Francine Prose

Short Story
F, 30s
Contemporary
Dramatic

*Zip and Jerry are cops. Zip responds to a call to
Jerry's house, and he encounters Jerry's wife,
Marianne.*

I'll bet you think Jerry's a normal guy, a sane, normal guy.
That's what everybody thinks (. . .) Even the guy's own
kids don't know how nuts he is. But trust me. The guy's
insane. (. . .)

Please, Zip. Don't Marianne me. You wouldn't believe
the crazy shit he says. (. . .) He goes into these jealous
rages, saying I'm some kind of witch, that I'm making
guys think about me, look at me, which wouldn't even
make sense even *if* we ever went anywhere where guys
could look at me. At some point tonight, probably the
minute you leave, he's going to come out with some para-
noid bullshit about how I brought you here with my
magic powers. (. . .)

If I was a witch, if I had magic powers, why would I
let my marriage get to the point (. . .) where I believe
that the fucker is trying to kill me? (. . .) You think a
witch would live like that? An abused wife lives like that.

Wuthering Heights
Emily Bronte

Novel
F, 30+
Classical
Dramatic

Catherine persuades Isabella Linton to put aside all thoughts of Heathcliff.

I wouldn't be you for a kingdom! Nelly, help me to convince her of her madness. Tell her what Heathcliff is: an unreclaimed creature, without refinement, without cultivation; an arid wilderness of furze and whinstone. I'd as soon put that little canary into the park on a winter's day, as recommend you to bestow your heart on him! It is deplorable ignorance of his character, child, and nothing else, which makes that dream enter your head. Pray, don't imagine that he conceals depths of benevolence and affection beneath a stern exterior! He's not a rough diamond—a pearl-containing oyster of a rustic: he's a fierce, pitiless, wolfish man. (. . .) [H]e'd crush you like a sparrow's egg, Isabella, if he found you a troublesome charge. I know he couldn't love a Linton; and yet he'd be quite capable of marrying your fortune and expectations (. . .). There's my picture: and I'm his friend — so much so, that had he thought seriously to catch you, I should, perhaps, have held my tongue, and let you fall into his trap. Banish him from your thoughts. He's a bird of bad omen: no mate for you.

Wuthering Heights
Emily Bronte

Novel
F, 40+
Classical
Dramatic

Mrs. Linton, proprietor of Thrushcross Grange, describes a recent fit of hysteria.

Nelly, I'll tell you what I thought, and what has kept recurring and recurring till I feared for my reason. I thought as I lay there, (. . .) that I was enclosed in the oak-panelled bed at home; and my heart ached with some great grief which, just waking, I could not recollect. I pondered, and worried myself to discover what it could be, and, most strangely, the whole last seven years of my life grew a blank! I did not recall that they had been at all. I was a child; my father was just buried (. . .). I cannot say why I felt so wildly wretched: it must have been temporary derangement; for there is scarcely cause. But, supposing at twelve years old I had been wrenched from the Heights, (. . .) and been converted at a stroke into Mrs. Linton, the lady of Thrushcross Grange, and the wife of a stranger: an exile, and outcast, thenceforth, from what had been my world. You may fancy a glimpse of the abyss where I groveled! (. . .) Oh, I'm burning! I wish I were out of doors! (. . .) I'm sure I should be myself were I once among the heather on those hills. Open the window again wide: fasten it open!

WYWH

Andrew Biss

Short Story
F, 55
Contemporary
Dramatic

*Eileen, a reclusive, middle-aged divorcee, recalls
the disappearance of her son.*

Billy disappeared twenty-six years ago—almost to the
day. He was seven-years-old. He just upped and disappeared . . . as if by magic.

They searched the neighborhood with a fine-toothed
comb, of course. Police, friends, neighbors—they all
pitched in. It was all over the news, on the television, in
the papers. Someone put his photograph on a flyer with a
telephone number you could call if you had any information. As time went on, his story began to disappear from
the news, the searches were finally called off, and the flyers became faded and torn and . . . blew away in the
wind.

A couple of years ago, as I was rummaging through
an old drawer looking for what I couldn't tell you now, I
came upon one of those old flyers. Gave me quite a start,
it did. Suddenly there was Billy looking up at me . . . with
that quizzical expression he sometimes had. I felt just like
I'd been run through with a sword. I couldn't move. I just
froze up, staring back at Billy's face and the four words in
big, black print written underneath it that simply said,
"Have you seen me?"

Yellow Pickled Radish

Patricia Jang

Essay
F, 20s
Contemporary
Seriocomic

A Korean-American female reflects on her cultural identity.

I was the only Asian in my grade school, a lone yellow, pickled radish floating in a bowl of chicken noodle soup. So I said "No!" to chili paste, dried cuttlefish, sticky rice, and kimchee, and said "Yes" to hot dogs, baloney and other American mystery meats.

When I was twelve, my parents announced that we were going to Korea for three weeks to visit relatives, I heard only one thing: kimchee for twenty-seven days.

Day Three in Seoul. (. . .) During breakfast, while extracting a mackerel bone from my gums, I noticed a box of cereal perched on the fridge.

"Mom! Look! They have CEREAL!"

Sure, the cereal tasted like the bastard son of Count Dracula but I didn't care. Hallelujah for native foodstuffs from my homeland! After my third bowl, I finally felt satiated for the first time in days.

An hour later, my family set off to the Korean Folk Village. Stuck inside my uncle's new Daewoo for hours in gridlocked traffic, I fought off successive waves of queasiness. Finally, we arrived at the Korean Folk Village, an occasion that demanded a photo. Before the photographer counted to three, a violent swell of nausea rose and I erupted. As my mother led me to the bathroom, I saw my aunt shaking her head — American food no good.

The Yellow Wallpaper
Charlotte Perkins Gilman

Short Story
F, 20s
Classical
Dramatic

1892. The narrator, a new mother, has been brought to a country house for a "rest-cure" by her husband; he selects for her the room with the yellow wall-paper, the former nursery, where the "windows are barred for little children" and the bed has been nailed to the floor.

Forbidden to write and think, prescribed for and infantilized, the narrator becomes increasingly dys-functional. She obsesses about the yellow wallpaper, in which she sees frightful patterns and an imprisoned female figure trying to emerge.

There is one marked peculiarity about this paper, a thing nobody seems to notice but myself.

At night in any kind of light, it becomes bars! The outside pattern I mean, and the woman behind it is as plain as can be.

I didn't realize for a long time what the thing was that showed behind, that dim sub-pattern, but now I am quite sure it is a woman. (. . .)

I think that woman gets out in the daytime!

And I'll tell you why—privately—I've seen her!

I can see her out of every one of my windows!

It is the same woman, I know, for she is always

creeping, and most women do not creep by daylight. I see her on that long road under the trees, creeping along, and when a carriage comes she hides under the blackberry vines.

I don't blame her a bit. It must be very humiliating to be caught creeping by daylight!

I always lock the door when I creep by daylight. I can't do it at night, for I know John would suspect something at once.

And John is so queer now, that I don't want to irritate him. I wish he would take another room! Besides, I don't want anybody to get that woman out at night but myself.

MEN'S MONOLOGUES

American Psycho

Bret Easton Ellis

Novel
M, 26
Contemporary
Dramatic

Speaking to his colleague on the way to work, successful, driven, caffeinated Timothy Price critiques New York and contemporary society. Circa 1990.

[T]he fact remains that no one gives a shit about their work, everybody hates their job, *I* hate my job, *you've* told me you hate yours. What do I do? Go back to Los Angeles? *Not* an alternative. I didn't transfer from UCLA to Stanford to put up with this? (. . .)

I hate to complain—I really do—about the trash, the garbage, the disease, about how filthy this city really is and *you* know and I know that it is a *sty. . .*(. . .) (*Pulls out today's newspaper.*) In one issue—in *one* issue—let's see here—strangled models, babies thrown from tenement rooftops, kids lolled in the subway, a Communist rally, Mafia boss wiped out, Nazis (. . .) baseball players with AIDS, more Mafia shit, gridlock, the homeless, various maniacs, (. . .) the cancellation of a soap opera, kids who broke into a zoo and tortured and burned various animals alive, more Nazis . . . and the joke is, the punch line *is*, it's all in this city—nowhere else, just here, it sucks, whoa wait, more Nazis, gridlock, gridlock, baby-sellers, black-market babies, AIDS babies, baby junkies, building collapses on baby, maniac baby, gridlock, bridge collapses—Why aren't you wearing the worsted navy blue blazer with the gray pants?

An HR Manager Responds To Alleged Infractions

Rick Stoeckel

Online Journal Entry
M, 30s+
Contemporary
Comic

Homeless Dress Friday: I thought this was a great way to boost morale, and it seemed a natural escalation from Casual Dress Fridays, but I was appalled to hear that it generated some negative feedback. People were encouraged to dress "as homeless as possible," bringing whatever props (booze bottles in paper bags, etc.) to set the mood. I don't feel the event was in any way "tasteless" or "insulting." I would understand my reproach if I had called the event "Leach on Society Friday" or "Dress Like a Bottom Feeder Day." Though accurate, the names are clearly not acceptable. The day was a success, and it even generated a windfall of change during smoke and coffee breaks from generous passersby outside the building. Regardless, the Pimps and Hos Dress Friday scheduled for next week has been called off.

Ass-Out Tuesday: This was voluntary; no one was forced to cut the back of their pants out. I believe people complained thinking it was some kind of mandatory event. I assure you, it was not. The confusion may have stemmed from me and a couple other guys pantsing Randy from the copy room. This was for other reasons.

Ass-Out Homeless Dress Monday: The merger of two great ideas. I expected this to be a big hit with the staff. The race riot that occurred that morning was, in my opinion, not preventable.

Babylon Revisited

F. Scott Fitzgerald

Short Story
M, 30s
Classical
Dramatic

1931. After the death of his wife, a husband, recovering from alcoholism and a mental breakdown, petitions his hostile in-laws for custody of his daughter, Honoria.

I suppose you know what I want to see you about—why I really came to Paris. I'm awfully anxious to have a home, and I'm awfully anxious to have Honoria in it. I appreciate your taking in Honoria for her mother's sake, but things have changed now—changed radically with me, and I want to ask you to reconsider the matter. It would be silly for me to deny that about three years ago I was acting badly—but that's all over. As I told you, I haven't had more than a drink a day for over a year, and I take that drink deliberately, so that the idea of alcohol won't get too big in my imagination. You see the idea? It's a sort of stunt I set myself. It keeps the matter in proportion. (. . .) Anyhow, I couldn't afford to drink in my position. The people I represent are more than satisfied with what I've done, and I'm bringing my sister over from Burlington to keep house for me, and I want awfully to have Honoria too. (. . .) I know she's fond of me and I know I'm able to take care of her and—well, there you are. How do you feel about it?

Balance Act

Ken Cormier

Short Story
M, 20+
Contemporary
Seriocomic

*A young man tries to reconcile the death of his
parents—among other things.*

The thing that weighs on me most heavily is the knowledge that negative forces can creep up on you and snap
you without a moment's notice, often in the middle of
your most cherished moments, always when you expect it
least. (. . .)

I do resent the fact that my parents were taken away
by something as stupid as a broken axle, pulling them off
a busy highway, over a guardrail, into oncoming traffic,
into a pickup truck, sixty miles an hour in the opposite
direction. The man in the pickup made it through with
only a big greenish-purple bruise where he was forced
into his seat belt. It's funny. A seat belt saves your life,
but it stripes you from shoulder to waist with broken
blood vessels and damaged tissue. All a guardrail does is
to provide you with a ramp into oncoming death. (. . .)
Seat belts should be arrested for assault and battery.
Guardrails should be booked on homicide charges. Cops
should be more polite, girls should just kiss you if they
want to kiss you, not dangle their faces two inches from
yours until you're just about crazy, and I should broaden
my sexual horizons.

Benito Cereno
Herman Melville

Short Story
M, 20s-30s
Classical
Dramatic

Babo is a ship captain's slave, about to shave his master's face with a razor. What we don't know is that Babo has secretly taken over the ship, and the captain fears Babo may slit his throat. Babo uses the razor, and his "master's" precarious position beneath it, to keep the captain from exposing the plot in front of the visiting Don Amasa.

Now, master.

You must not shake so, Master. See, Don Amasa, master always shakes when I shave him. And yet master knows I never yet have drawn blood, though it's true if master will shake so I may some of these times. Now master. And now, Don Amasa, please go on with your talk about the gale, and all that; master can hear, and be-tween times, master can answer. (. . .)

(Babo "accidentally" cuts his master.) See, master—you shook so—here's Babo's first blood. *(Offering him a cloth.)* But answer Don Amasa, please, master, while I wipe this ugly stuff off the razor, and strop it again. (. . .)

Be patient, *señor*, these fits do not last long; master will soon be himself.

(Babo strops the razor, smiling.)

Bob Kennedy, 56; Akron, Ohio

Eric Feezell

Essay
M, 56
Contemporary
Comic

This is from Feezell's "Anticlimactic Retellings of Near-Death Experiences Rejected for Inclusion in a Forthcoming Talk-Show Segment Entitled 'Life, Death, and Beyond.'"

Last September, my heart stopped. For ten minutes I was clinically dead. *Dead*, people. And you know how they say that when you die you sort of rise above yourself, and you're floating there, looking down on your lifeless vessel, and your family is outside the room crying hysterically while the doctors are frantically doing everything they can to resuscitate you, and your spirit version of yourself has this huge decision to make—you know, like, a "Should I stay or should I go?" type of thing?

Yeah, it wasn't like that at all. I don't recall if my family was even there. Come to think of it, I can't remember a single detail about the whole ordeal—just waking up with that goddamn tube in my ding-dong.

The Boss Is Dead

Ron Pullins

Novella
M, 35+
Contemporary
Seriocomic

*A supervisor tells his staff about a great grill man,
Baptiste, who is now derelict.*

Baptiste was a grill man. None better. I remember the
night of the big football game. We're hometown, behind
twenty to three. And the manager—his son is quarter-
back—announces if we win, then its two-fer-one at Inter-
burger.

Two-fer-one! Half price is bad, but two for one is
twice the work. And . . . we won! Second half, four
touchdowns, boom, boom, boom, boom. And field goal
wins the game. Here they come, and old Baptiste and me
are alone in the store. Hundreds—kids, parents, the town
we were playing—all ordering two-fers.

Baptiste, moving like a bug in hot grease, takes the
back line, fries, wraps and garnishes. He never burns a
hamburger, never burns a bun. He is magnificent. I'm up
front, I take the orders, sometimes thirty, forty deep, five,
eight, ten orders at once, and I sell out—fries, shakes,
cheese, meat, pies, dogs. In the end, we only have grilled
cheese to sell, no cokes, no shakes, no coffee!

People stopped coming just for the food. They came
for us. To see the two of us. They came back for weeks,
just to say, "Them two, they're the ones."

The Boss Is Dead

Ron Pullins

Novella
M, 25+
Contemporary
Seriocomic

A supervisor reminds the night manager how to cook the perfect fried potato.

The perfect fry is perfectly frozen, then dropped immediately—fully frozen—into shortening of the exact temperature to sear the outer layer, scald it, seal it shut. Nothing escapes, nothing in, nothing out, and inside this fry the moisture is trapped—moisture that cannot escape, cannot leave, finds the front sealed, the back sealed, both sides closed in, trapped in this oppressive heat, and the heat rises, rises, turns suddenly to steam—purifying, scalding steam that races the length of the potato, and back again, but there is no escape. We are precise about what we want, so there is no error possible, no error at all, and only one outcome—the perfect fry. Foolproof. Unless we have a fool running our stores. Unless, and only unless, we have a manager who fails to change the . . . grease. We have precise instructions in the manual, do we not, about our shortening, and we explain, is it not true, that shortening, over time, over cooking, after so many fries and frost and water and time, no longer seals the fry instantly, traps the moisture, keeps the shortening out? Instead fries in old shortening, worn out shortening, are boiled like so much spaghetti in water. Boiled fries. Soggy, greasy, limp fries. Grease that runs out when you squeeze them. Grease that runs down my hand. Greasy limp-dick fries like these.

Brunch

Daniel Drennan

Essay
M, 30s
Contemporary
Comic

Ah . . . friends.

Every Saturday morning for the past few years, my friend Robyn has called me to ask about brunch; the fact of the matter is that we might as well just go to the exact same restaurant at the exact same time every Saturday, only that would be too simple. Every Saturday Robyn calls and says "what are you doing?" and I say "being woken up by a phone call" and she says "what are you doing today?" and I say "I don't know" and she says "you want to have brunch?" and I say "okay" and she says "where?" and I say "the exact same place we go every Saturday" and she says "what time?" and I say "the exact same time we have it every Saturday" and I don't think it is possible for two people in their mid-thirties to act more like ninety-year-old women whose only reason for living is to pester one another.

Burger King
Mark Hillringhouse

Creative Nonfiction
M, 40s
Contemporary
Comic

*Cost of filling your gas tank to get to your first
day on the job: $3.00. Photo of you in your
Burger King uniform: $1.00. Almost burning
the place down: priceless.*

My college roommate and I came to work [at Burger King]. My friend got fries; I got meat. I was told to stand in one place and to put the buns on this belt, the meat on the other. Problem was my roommate and I dropped two hits of "Windowpane" LSD before we got here, and I was starting to feel the change. The manager left, and the assistant manager left, and we were in charge. The first customers started coming in. This was before the drive-up window. I was loading burger patties onto the flame-broiler conveyor belt, buns onto the toaster conveyor belt trying to remember which went where. The acid was taking hold: the bright lights on the white walls glared the red color of the tile floor, all geometric patterns and colors were colliding. The buns were bursting into flame. The meat came out a dripping raw mass of fat. A customer yelled, "What the hell is this crap!" The kids working the counter got scared. One of them left. My roommate was deep-frying napkins, ketchup bottles, saying "Man look at this!" He even deep-fried his Burger

King hard hat. I can still hear his maniacal laughter. I was pressed up against the plate glass window holding two fistfuls of meat wiping streaks of fat on the glass. "Look at the patterns," I yelled. My face was on the glass. I saw a customer come up to the door, turn around and run back to his car.

Charles Boyer Is on the Loose

Barbara Lindsay

Short Story
M, 60s
Contemporary
Comic

After forty years, Gus' wife, Loretta has decided that they need more romance in their marriage. Here Gus tries to explain his attempts to satisfy Loretta's unexpected desire.

So Loretta tells me she wants romance, like I'm supposed to know what she means. So I say, "OK. What do you mean?" And she goes on about if she has to tell me, it's not romance, because with romance, it just happens spur of the moment. Which at least lets me off the hook for planning a trip to Hawaii. Only this business about how she can't tell me what to do, I have to think of it myself, this seems unfair when it was her brought it up in the first place. Now I'm all confused and getting sort of pan-icky, only with all this talk about romance, panic is feel-ing a little like getting turned on, which in my mind is a good thing, because I don't care what they say when they talk about romance, what they mean is sex. So that's what we do. We have sex. Only this is the romantic part. We do it on the floor. She says afterward that isn't what she meant. But she made me chicken rice for dinner, and she was humming while she did the dishes. So I'm think-ing, "Hey. Romance. You know. Not bad."

Checkpoint
Nicholas Baker

Novel
M, 30s-40s
Contemporary
Seriocomic

It's 2004, and Jay has decided to assassinate the president of the United States. In trying to convince his friend, Ben, to join him, he explains how he arrived at his decision.

The weird thing about this administration, actually, is that the big guys in it are historical figures already. They've lurched back to life.

It's as if these rusted hulks, these zombies, have fought their way back up out of the peat bogs where they've been lying, and they're stumbling around with grubs scurrying in and out of their noses and they're going "We—are—your—advisers."

I mean they're there, physically in the White House, making decisions—Dick Cheney!

Oh, he's hunched, man, the corruption has completely hunched and gnarled him. His mouth is pulled totally over on one side of his face. It's really—And the apple-cheeked boys with their cruel mouths, starstruck, I swear they fall in love with these drugstore cowboys. George W. Bush, J. Danforth Quayle. Surrounded by fawners who want to Serve Our Leader. Soon they're going to discover some hormonal thing that leads to right-wing behavior, some very specific deficiency combined with an overdose. You end up mean-spirited, with a high, whiny voice.

Checkpoint

Nicholas Baker

Novel
M, 30s-40s
Contemporary
Seriocomic

*It's 2004, and Ben has learned his friend intends to
assassinate the president of the United States and
needs Ben's help to pull it off.*

Yeah, but see, what you're doing here, though, and I say
this as gently as I can, is you're using me. I didn't know
when you called that you wanted to tape our discussion
prior to killing the president of the United States. I did
not know that. If I had known that I would have said, No
thank you, I'm going to be scanning some transparencies
and I think you better call somebody else, because I'm not
going to drive to Washington to hear the gory details.

What you said was "I really need to talk to you."
And I thought, Oh, OK, he really needs to talk to me.
Sounds like the poor guy is in a crisis state. We've all
been in states of despair. But, but. I didn't know that you
wanted to talk to me about doing *this*. I don't like this.
And then, this whole thing that you just laid on me, that
if I call the law you're going to whip out a firearm and all
that—I don't like it. I'm not sure that I want to be threat-
ened with science, with being shot in the leg, it's not en-
joyable. I'm not going to tolerate it, in fact. I'm going to
walk out right now.

Christopher Hitchens Visits St. Margaret's School for Young Women, Where He Discovers Little Girls Aren't Funny, Either

Kate Kershner

Online Journal Entry
M, 30+
Contemporary
Comic

The skit began with a markedly funny premise: two women discussing sports. Dreary results. Sarah and Emily from Ms. Franklin's fourth-grade class recited the most elementary—and frankly grating—dialogue imaginable. Apparently, the girls wanted the audience to believe that a character by the name of "Who" was playing the position of first base, that "What" manned second, and that "I Don't Know" covered third for a particular baseball team. (. . .) Even I couldn't follow the damn thing, and I'm a man who is remarkably clever. It seemed a shame that the girls received a standing ovation for their dismal performance while boys all over the country are given detention for trying to light their farts on fire during recess, which is fucking hysterical.

If you ever desire to see a large group of dour young girls staring humorlessly at you, go to Mrs. Garvey's sixth-grade class during sex ed and make a vagina joke. But don't do the one about the very hungry caterpillar, because Mrs. Garvey will make you stop halfway through. Not that it matters, as these girls were entirely preoccupied with asking the most obvious questions about their biology. How badly do cramps hurt? How long does a period last? Should they have gotten theirs yet? Who the fuck cares, when surrounded by the hilarity of the reproductive system? When Mrs. Garvey, pressed for time, asked if they could "handle doing the male anatomy" tomorrow, no one even batted an eyelash, even with my prompt and loud guffaw. (. . .) Like I said, women just aren't funny.

Clowns

Kevin Brown

Short Story
M, 35+
Contemporary
Seriocomic

The tears of a clown.

Dumb bitch. Married to her for thirteen years and one day she up and decides her life is boring and wants to be a painter (. . .) And now she pulls this shit. That's what I get for marrying a bitch whose family tree is really a family wreath.

Me, now I'm a clown. Literally. My clown name is "Clyde." "Clyde the Clown." I work birthdays and bat mitzvahs. Hospitals. An occasional wedding. Even did a funeral once. My makeup's a rip-off of Bozo the Clown, and if face paint is considered copyrighted property, I could be facing a lawsuit.

My act is the usual—I squirt water from a little sunflower on my lapel, do a little stand-up routine. Dabble in a bit of magic. Last week I purchased the book *The Magic's Not Real But Who Cares?* and learned how to stick a rabbit in a hat. Then there's the little animal balloons. I make dogs out of balloons. Make cats and giraffes out of balloons. Make elephants and hearts out of balloons. It doesn't pay much but I take clowning seriously. And now Bitch's trying to make a fool out of me.

The Country Husband

John Cheever

Short Story
M, early 20s
Contemporary
Seriocomic

1950s. Clayton Thomas, made humorless and affected through a series of family misfortunes, accepts a cup of coffee from Julia and Francis Weed, and fills them in on his plans for the future.

[Well,] I'd like to work for a publisher, but everyone tells me there's nothing doing. (. . .) (. . .) Uncle Charlie might get me into a bank, and that would be good for me. I need the discipline. I have a long way to go in forming my character. I have some terrible habits. I talk too much. I think I ought to take vows of silence. I ought to try not to speak for a week, and discipline myself. I've thought of making a retreat at one of the Episcopalian monasteries, but I don't like Trinitarianism. (. . .) I'm engaged to be married. Of course, I'm not old enough or rich enough to have my engagement observed or respected or anything, but I bought a simulated emerald for Anne Murchison with the money I made cutting lawns this summer. We're going to be married as soon as she finishes school. (. . .) We're going to have a large family. (. . .) Oh, she's wonderful, Mr. and Mrs. Weed, and we have so much in common. We like all the same things. We sent out the same Christmas card last year without planning it, and we both have an allergy to tomatoes, and our eyebrows grow together in the middle. Well, good night.

Crime and Punishment

Fyodor Dostoevsky, Translator Constance
Garnett

Novel
M, 30s+
Classical
Dramatic

*Marmeladov, deep in his cups,
bemoans his sorry lot.*

Well, so be it, I am a pig, but she is a lady! I have the
semblance of a beast, but Katerina Ivanovna, my spouse
is a person of education and an officer's daughter.
Granted, granted, I am a scoundrel, but she is a woman
of a noble heart, full of sentiments, refined by education.
And yet . . . oh, if only she felt for me! (. . .) And yet, although I realise that when she pulls my hair she only does
it out of pity—for I repeat without being ashamed, she
pulls my hair, young man, but, my God, if she would but
once. . . . But no, no! It's all in vain and it's no use talking! No use talking! (. . .) . . . such is my fate and I am a
beast by nature! Do you know, sir, do you know, I have
sold her very stockings for drink? Not her shoes—that
would be more or less in the order of things, but her
stockings, her stockings I have sold for drink! Her mohair
shawl I sold for drink, a present to her long ago, her own
property, not mine; and we live in a cold room and she
caught cold this winter and has begun coughing and spitting blood too. We have three little children and Katerina
Ivanovna is at work from morning till night; she is scrub-
bing and cleaning and washing the children, for she's been

used to cleanliness from a child. But her chest is weak and she has a tendency to consumption and I feel it! Do you suppose I don't feel it? And the more I drink the more I feel it. That's why I drink too. I try to find sympathy and feeling in drink. . . . I drink so that I may suffer twice as much!

Damn!
H. L. Mencken

Essay
M, 30+
Classical
Comic

An attempted justification for infidelity.

I have said that 95 per cent of married men are faithful.
I believe the real proportion is nearer 99 per cent. What
women mistake for infidelity is usually no more than van-
ity. Every man likes to be regarded as a devil of a fellow,
and particularly by his wife. On the one hand, it diverts
her attention from his more genuine shortcomings, and
on the other hand, it increases her respect for him. More-
over, it gives her a chance to win the sympathy of other
women, and so satisfies that craving for martyrdom
which is perhaps woman's strongest characteristic. A
woman who never has any chance to suspect her husband
feels cheated and humiliated. She is in the position of
those patriots who are induced to enlist for a war by pictures of cavalry charges, and then find themselves told to
wash the general's underwear.

Daniel Hennessy, 79;
Helena, Montana
Eric Feezell

Essay
M, 79
Contemporary
Comic

This is from Feezell's "Anticlimactic Retellings of Near-Death Experiences Rejected for Inclusion in a Forthcoming Talk-Show Segment Entitled 'Life, Death, and Beyond.'"

I still can't believe I came out of the coma. Christ, nine months—everyone thought I was a goner.

People always ask me now, what was it like? You know, being that close to death for so long. You know what I tell them? It was *boring as hell*. All this damn modern medical technology and the doctors couldn't figure some way to mainline some television programs into my neurobiological network or something? Some Sudoku? I mean, pull the dang plug already. Anything but that godforsaken soundless black void!

Jesus, talk about a crappy-ass nine months.

David Caruso Scolds His Cat About Its Lackadaisical Litter-box Use

Brian Graham

Essay
M, 35+
Contemporary
Comic

Now, Bosco. You know what you did was wrong. What you did was improper. It was inconsiderate. But you didn't think about that, did you? You thought you could get away with it. But you forgot the most important thing. You forgot that the only thing that matters is evidence.

Or perhaps you thought I'd go easy on you. That all this could be solved with the gift of a recently deceased bird on my doorstep. But you are wrong. Dead wrong. (. . .) You can purr all you like, but I know that the purr is a lie. I trusted you to use the litter box. The rule was clear and indisputable, and yet you broke it. Again and again. Right on the kitchen floor.

You made a choice. And you know what they say, Bosco: "You lie down with the devil, you wake up in hell." So next time you decide to relieve yourself, think about the consequences. Act carefully. Because the thin ice you are treading on is cracking beneath your paws. And when you fall into the freezing water, I'm not going to be the one to bend down and save you.

Now get off my lap.

Decker Moody, Swimming Pool Salesman

Chuck Strangward

Online Journal Entry
M, 20s-30s
Contemporary
Comic

I don't have anything against pools that have vinyl liners, except for one thing: They suck. Even Shamu doesn't swim in a vinyl-lined pool. The only time I've ever used a vinyl liner was when I built my wife a turtle pond. And it leaked. One day I found the turtles scraping along the bottom, freaked out of their minds. Imagine coming home and finding your kids in a similar predicament. Not pretty.

Here's what you need to know about Decker Moody. He's honest. Not because he's telling you he's honest, but because he is, after all, me, and lying in the third person would be idiotic and pointless, even if I were telling you the truth, which I am.

(. . .) Owning a pool is about living life to its fullest, about existing in the moment. (. . .) You can't have a nervous breakdown while sitting in a spa. Pools often widen one's social circle, and I've seen them bring families together, even mend broken marriages. A pool can replenish the marrow of your soul. Then again, lots of people drown. Decker Moody is not God.

The Devil and Daniel Webster

Stephen Vincent Benet

Short Story
M, 20+
Classical
Dramatic

"It's a story they tell in the border country, where Massachusetts joins Vermont and New Hampshire."

They said, when [Dan'l Webster] stood up to speak, stars and stripes came right out in the sky, and once he spoke against a river and made it sink into the ground. They said, when he walked the woods with his fishing rod, Killall, the trout would jump out of the streams right into his pockets, for they knew it was no use putting up a fight against him; and when he argued a case, he could turn on the harps of the blessed and the shaking of the earth underground. (. . .) A man with a mouth like a mastiff, a brow like a mountain and eyes like burning anthracite—that was Dan'l Webster in his prime. And the biggest case he argued never got written down in the books, for he argued it against the devil, nip and tuck and no holds barred. (. . .)

They say that whenever the devil comes near Marshfield, even now, he gives it a wide berth. And he hasn't been seen in the state of New Hampshire from that day to this. I'm not talking about Massachusetts or Vermont.

The Devil Wears Prada

Lauren Weisberger

Novel
M, 30s
Contemporary
Comic

Meet Nigel, no-last-name. He's flamboyant. He likes italics and exclamation marks. He talks in caps.

YOU! STAND UP SO I CAN GET A LOOK AT YOU! (. . .) WELL! WHO DO WE HAVE HEEEEERE? YOU'RE PRETTY, BUT TOO WHOLESOME. AND THE OUTFIT DOES NOTHING FOR YOU! (. . .) KNEE-HIGH BOOTS? WITH A KNEE-LENGTH SKIRT? ARE YOU KIDDING ME? BABY GIRL, IN CASE YOU'RE UNAWARE—IN CASE YOU MISSED THE BIG, BLACK SIGN BY THE DOOR—THIS IS *RUNWAY* MAGAZINE, THE FUCKING *HIIPPEST* MAGAZINE ON EARTH. ON EARTH! BUT NO WORRIES, HONEY, NIGEL WILL GET RID OF THAT JERSEY MALL-RAT LOOK YOU'VE GOT GOING SOON ENOUGH. (. . .) SOON ENOUGH, SWEETIE, I PROMISE YOU, BECAUSE YOU'RE GOOD RAW MA-TERIAL. NICE LEGS, GREAT HAIR, AND NOT FAT. I CAN WORK WITH NOT FAT. SOON ENOUGH, SWEETIE.

The Devil Wears Prada

Lauren Weisberger

Novel
M, 30s
Contemporary
Comic

Nigel, loud and high-pitched, does his fashion police thang all over James.

I WANT YOU TO MARCH YOUR WAY BACK N THERE AND TELL THE GIRLS WHAT YOU WERE THINKING WHEN YOU PUT THAT SHMATA ON THIS MORNING! (. . .)

LOVE THAT TOP? YOU THINK I LOVE THAT FRATTY, BAY-JOCK LOOK YOU'VE GOT GOING? JAMES, YOU NEED TO RETHINK HER, OK? OK? (. . .)

BABY BOY, FASHION IS NOT FOR ADVERTISING YOUR FAVE SEX ACTS ON YOUR SHIRT. UNH-UNH, NO IT'S NOT! YOU WANNA SHOW A LITTLE SKIN? THAT'S HOT! YOU WANNA SHOW SOME THOSE TIGHT, YOUNG CURVES OF YOURS? *THAT'S* HOT. CLOTHING IS NOT FOR TELLING THE WORLD WHAT POSITION YOU PREFER, BOYFRIEND. NOW DO YOU UNDERSTAND? (. . .)

DON'T "NIGEL" ME, HONEY, GO TALK TO JEFFY AND TELL HIM I SENT YOU. TELL HIM TO GIVE YOU THE NEW CALVIN TANK WE CALLED IN FOR THE MIAMI SHOOT. IT'S THE ONE THAT GORGEOUS BLACK MODEL—OH MY, HE'S AS

TASTY AS A THICK, CHOCOLATE MILK SHAKE—IS
ASSIGNED TO WEAR. GO ON NOW, SHOO. (. . .)
   MIRANDA PRIESTLY! TAKE THAT RAG OFF
THIS SECOND. THAT DRESS MAKES YOU LOOK
LIKE A SLUT! A COMMON WHORE!

Do-It-Yourself

Phineas Mollod and Jason Tesauro

Essay
M, 20+
Contemporary
Comic

This selection is from *The Modern Gentleman,*
"a guide to essential manners, savvy & vice."
Think of Alfred, the butler advising young Bruce
Wayne. Add a little James Bond in training.
Top with Hugh Hefner on a good day. Shake,
don't stir. From Chapter Three: Wooing.

As table-manner expert Marjabelle Young Stewart's credo states: Stroke the meat, don't saw it. The authors will not provide a guiding hand regarding the "solitary rumba," "han solos," "white knuckler," or "back-stroke roulette." We assume a gentleman has honed this skill through years of trial and little error. We will not chair a panel concerning the alleged myopic effects from "hand-to-gland combat" or "driving the skin bus." Rather, the following concerns the ins and outs of "fisting one's mister" during a grounded relationship, when sexual relations and intimacy are touchstones.

Certain instances require an immediate "hand shandy." No matter how stupendous a sex life, the occasional, undeniable fantasy ought be slaked. Giving in to your personal carnality infrequently keeps it a stolen pleasure. This rare practice will not hamstring award-winning romps or tarnish your moral fiber.

"Giving Yul Brynner a high five" is a sexual supplement and a mild affirmation of autonomy that's as right as rain. No main squeezer, however wonderful, can oblige all needs, all the time. When in love, "hitchhiking under the big top" appears somehow fresh. So "meet your right-hand man" and "pan for white gold," because cheating with yourself is not cheating.

Down There
Laura Jacqmin

Short Story
M, 14-18
Contemporary
Seriocomic

Now that Joe has convinced his older sister to go to Antarctica in search of their mother, he is wary of being left alone.

You're not even allowed to sweat down there in Antarctica, did you know that? It's one of the rules.

You'd better get used to the rules, fast, or it'll be bad for you.

They'll say, she's not a team player.

They'll say, she'd better go back north, to the easy life. They'll make you eat seven meals a day to bulk up, and crates of chocolate bars, and gallons of tequila with frozen lemon that you stick in your cheek and bite down on, like a dental X-ray.

Your teeth will get hard in the wind, and your face will turn all angles.

Everyone has to be slaves to the scientists because they're the only ones who know how to melt the snow. They'll make you hike, and pitch tents, and sleep close to strangers, and they'll talk at you all the time to remind themselves that they're still alive.

There might be bears.

Big, white bears.

Bears made of sleet.

Bears carved out of glaciers, with ice teeth, and snow jaws and cold, dense fur.

Hiding in the permafrost.

Waiting.

I —

I don't know what else to say.

I don't know how to convince you. To stay.

I wish I knew a song to sing you. Because down there, there'll be no singing. Only wind.

The Fall of the House of Usher
Edgar Allen Poe

Short Story
M, 30s
Classical
Dramatic

Descending into madness over the guilt of having buried his sister alive in the family vault, Usher confesses to a visitor, Ethelred.

Now hear it?—yes, I hear it, and *have* heard it. Long—long—long—many minutes, many hours, many days, have I heard it—yet I dared not—oh, pity me, miserable wretch that I am!—I dared not—I *dared* not speak! *We have put her living in the tomb!* Said I not that my senses were acute? I *now* tell you that I heard her first feeble movements in the hollow coffin. I heard them many, many days ago—yet I dared not—*I dared not speak!* And now—to-night—Ethelred—ha! ha!—the breaking of the hermit's door, and the death-cry of the dragon, and the clangor of the shield—say, rather, the rending of her coffin, and the grating of the iron hinges of her prison, and her struggles within the coppered archway of the vault! Oh! whither shall I fly? Will she not be here anon? Is she not hurrying to upbraid me for my haste? Have I not heard her footstep on the stair? Do I not distinguish that heavy and horrible beating of her heart? Madman! (. . .) *Madman! I tell you that she now stands without the door!*

Fana!
Thomas M. Kelly

Short Story
M, 25-35
Dramatic
Contemporary

*Zhev, a black guard of mixed Jewish/Muslim her-
itage, is trapped with a suicide bomber among rub-
ble and victims. He does not know the man he
speaks to is the bomber.*

As a boy of seventeen I joined the Israeli Defense Force.
I felt as if I was embarking on a sacred mission of valor,
courage, and bravery: to defend and protect my country.
Instead, I found myself violating the dignity of Palestinians, tearing up the personal documents of men as old as
my grandfather. Pointing my weapons at children.

In the days before the Gulf War many Palestinians
were fleeing Kuwait. We reservists met them at the border, looked away in embarrassment and disgust as we saw
conscripts ripping apart children's comforters, and empty-
ing their mother's bags of what remained of their lives in
search of weapons and explosives. We wanted to find
contraband so that we could arrest them.

I saw my fellow reservists sink into the vilest of
human beings. I heard stories of kidnappings and beatings. The beatings did not stop at the spilling of blood.
As the level of insanity, hatred, and violence for the sake
of retribution grew I became more disenchanted with the
military. I became more passive. I did not like myself

then. That young bravery, courage, and pride of service turned to self-hatred. Passivity and self-hatred turned to resistance. I still wanted to serve my Israel. But not this way. Not like this.

Frankenstein
Mary Shelley

Novel
M, 20s+
Classical
Dramatic

The creature speaks to his creator.

All men hate the wretched. How, then, must I be hated, who am miserable beyond all living things! Yet you, my creator, detest and spurn me, thy creature, to whom thou art bound by ties only dissoluble by the annihilation of one of us. You propose to kill me. How dare you sport thus with life? Do your duty toward me, and I will do mine toward you and the rest of mankind. If you will comply with my conditions, I will leave them and you at peace, but if you refuse I will glut the maw of death, until it be satiated with the blood of your remaining friends. (. . .) Life, although it may only be an accumulation of anguish, is dear to me, and I will defend it. Remember, thou hast made me more powerful than thyself. My height is superior to thine, my joints more supple. But I will not be tempted to set myself in opposition to thee. I am thy creature and I will be even mild and docile to my natural lord and king, if thou wilt also perform thy part, the which thou owest me. Oh, Frankenstein, be not equitable to every other and trample upon me alone, to whom thy justice, and even thy clemency and affection, is most due. Remember that I am thy creature.

The Girls in Their Summer Dresses

Irwin Shaw

Short Story
M, 35+
Contemporary
Dramatic

Speaking to his wife, a husband defends his habit of looking at other women. They sit in a bar on a lazy New York Sunday, sipping brandies.

I love the way women look. One of the things I like best about New York is the battalions of women. When I first came to New York from Ohio that was the first thing I noticed, the million wonderful women, all over the city. I walked around with my heart in my throat. (. . .)

I'm older now (. . .), putting on a little fat, and I still love to walk along Fifth Avenue at three o'clock (. . .). They're all out then, shopping, in their furs and their crazy hats, everything all concentrated from all over the world into seven blocks—. (. . .)

I like the girls in the offices. Neat, with their eyeglasses, smart, chipper, knowing what everything is about. I like the girls on Forty-fourth Street at lunchtime, the actresses, all dressed up on nothing a week. I like the salesgirls in the stores, paying attention to you first because you're a man, leaving lady customers waiting. (. . .)

I feel as though I'm at a picnic in this city. I like to sit near the women in the theaters, the famous beauties who've taken six hours to get ready and look it. And the young girls at the football games, with the red cheeks, and when the warm weather comes, the girls in their summer dresses. (. . .) That's the story.

Havris & Eli

Ken Cormier

Short Story
M, 40+
Contemporary
Dramatic

Two dysfunctional men fall head over heels for each other's insecurities.

[A]ll I can think about is Eli, the guy I work with at the ice cream shop. He's so thin and he's gorgeous and he always talks about old television shows and smiles at me. (. . .)

On our first date he told me he loved me and that he knew it was stupid to feel that way on a first date and that I couldn't possibly feel the same way and that he probably ruined any chance I had for loving him by making such a strong statement so early in our relationship. I said, "No, I love you, too." And I bought him some French fries and a seltzer water at the Dairy Queen. He kept smiling at me but every once in a while he'd go into these crying fits that were so violent he could barely speak a word. And when he managed to say anything it would be something like "everything's ruined" or "I can't keep going" or just "help me."

But it was nice, in a way, to have someone so emotionally distraught around. I've never been able to handle anything in my life, but next to Eli I seemed secure.

The Hope of All

Barbara Lindsay

Short Story
M, 20s
Contemporary
Dramatic

Chico is a borderline gangbanger who is trying to be straight up but is drawn to the world of violence, rebellion, and lawlessness. Here he confides to his homey, Nandez, that the birth of his first child has left him with a new and uncomfortable perspective.

This baby, man, she don't even look like a person. I look at her, I just see this brown, wet thing, kind of ugly and out of focus. I don't even feel connected to her. I know she's mine and everything, I mean, I was there when she got planted, and I know it was that time because that time was not like any other time. That was the time we made a baby, man, no mistake about it. Juana was so happy and I just thought, "Oh shit. We made a baby. Now what do I do?" Because I don't think I got what she's going to need. You know? That's my blood in her. And I put a lot of shit into my blood, man. I put beer and tequila and a hundred thousand plates of chorizo in there. I put heroin in there. I put sex with other women in there. And now it's in her. Esperanza. What am I supposed to do with that? I already fucked her up, and she ain't even a person yet.

Humoresque

Fannie Hurst

Short Story
M, 20s
Classical
Dramatic

1919. A gifted musician defends a decision made to enlist and go to war.

We *have* got a fight with some one! With autocracy! Only this time it happens to be Hunnish autocracy. You should know it, Mamma—oh, you should know it deeper down in you than any of us, the fight our family right here has got with autocracy! We should be the first to want to avenge Belgium!

The way you and Papa were beaten out of your country—there's not a day in your life you don't curse it without know it! Every time we three boys look at your son and our brother Mannie, born an—an imbecile—because of autocracy, we know what we're fighting for. We know. You know, too. Look at him over there, even before he was born, ruined by autocracy! Know what I'm fighting for? Why, this whole family knows! What's music, what's art, what's life itself in a world without freedom? Every time, Ma, you get to think we've got a fight with no one, all you have to do is look at our poor Mannie. He's the answer. He's the answer.

The Hunchback of Notre Dame

Victor Hugo, Translator Isabel F. Hapgood

Novel
M, 40+
Classical
Dramatic

A priest agonizes over a young woman.

Oh! Have pity upon me! You think yourself unhappy; alas! alas! you know not what unhappiness is. Oh! to love a woman! to be a priest! to be hated! to love with all the fury of one's soul; to feel that one would give for the least of her smiles, one's blood, one's vitals, one's fame, one's salvation, one's immortality and eternity, this life and the other; to clasp her night and day in one's dreams and one's thoughts, and to behold her in love with the trappings of a soldier and to have nothing to offer her but a priest's dirty cassock, which will inspire her with fear and disgust! To be present with one's jealousy and one's rage, while she lavishes on a miserable, blustering imbecile, treasures of love and beauty! To behold that body whose form burns you, that bosom which possesses so much sweetness, that flesh palpitate and blush beneath the kisses of another! Oh heaven! to love her foot, her arm, her shoulder, to think of her blue veins, of her brown skin, until one writhes for whole nights together on the pavement of one's cell, and to behold all those caresses which one has dreamed of, end in torture! Child! torture me with one hand, but caress me with the other! Have pity, young girl! Have pity upon me!

I Learned The Science Of Melancholy and the Art Of Regret in the Backseat Of Her Father's Old Car

J. J. Steinfeld

Short Short Story
M, 45-55
Contemporary
Dramatic

The bittersweet memory of a troubled young woman haunts a middle-aged man.

I was sixteen, looked fourteen, she was seventeen, looked like a movie star except with a scholar's knowledge of Sylvia Plath's poetry. I had never even heard of Sylvia Plath until she read me the high-school essay she had written on Plath's poetry. I told her she could talk so poetic sometimes, and she told me she thought kissing was poetic, liked to kiss me, more than any of the others. She showed me how she had kissed men older than either of our immigrant fathers: a math teacher with blond hair and tiny ears who could do square roots with his pants down; a man who worked a camera on a local TV news show and gave her an autographed picture; she even kissed her uncle's best friend who had lost an eye in a sudden bloody fight with a skinny jealous prizefighter who had been on the cover of a glossy boxing magazine. She showed me how she had recited nursery rhymes with two old men during a thunderstorm—brothers who had shared guilt and hatred like a thick milk shake in an ugly little diner and called her mama, our dearest mama, even if she was only seventeen(. . .). She showed me how to suspend language; she showed me a beautiful knife that is quicker than poetry. One of these men she was going to meet again that very evening, in that very same vehicle, she told me, and while he studied her dress and asked as usual if she was wearing pretty panties, she was going to slash her name into the headlines. That night I wrote my first poem, about melancholy and regret, about almost tasting love, about the backseat of her father's old car, and then turned on the TV news to see if she was telling the truth.

I'm a Fool
Sherwood Anderson

Short Story
M, 20s
Classical
Comic

*1922. A stable boy kicks himself for trying to impress
a girl by pretending he's a hotshot.*

Sometimes I hope I have cancer and die. I guess you know
what I mean. We went in the launch across the bay to the
train, and it was dark too. She whispered and said it was
like she and I could get out of the boat and walk on the
water, and it sounded foolish, but I knew what she meant.

And then quick, we were right at the depot, and there
was a big gang of yaps, and crowded and milling around
like cattle, and how could I tell her? "It won't be long because you'll write and I'll write to you." That's all she
said.

I got a chance like a hay barn afire. A swell chance I
got.

And maybe she would write me, and the letter would
come back, and stamped on the front it, "There ain't any
such guy," or something like that, whatever they stamp
on a letter that way.

And me trying to pass myself off for a big bug and a
swell—to her, as decent a little body as God ever made.
Craps almighty. A swell chance I got.

I'm a Fool
Sherwood Anderson

Short Story
M, 20s
Classical
Comic

1922. A stable boy tries to impress a girl by pretending he's a hotshot, and when she falls for him, finds he is unable to admit the truth. As her train leaves the station, he kicks himself.

Socks almighty, what was the use? Did you ever see such a fool?

I'll tell you what—if I had an arm broke right now or a train had run over my foot—I wouldn't go to no doctor at all. I'd go set down and let her hurt and hurt—that's what I'd do.

I'll tell you what—if I hadn't a drunk that booze I'd never been such a boob as to go tell such a lie—that couldn't never be made straight to a lady like her.

I wish I had that fellow right here that had on a Windsor tie and carried a cane. I'd smash him for fair. Gosh darn his eyes. He's a big fool—that's what he is.

And if I'm not another you just go find me one and I'll quit working and be a bum and give him my job. I don't care nothing for working and earning money and saving it for no such boob as myself.

Imagine Kissing Pete

John O'Hara

Short Story
M, 44
Contemporary
Dramatic

1960. During the Depression, Bobbie married Pete on the rebound, and Pete has always resented it. After treating Bobbie badly for twenty years, Pete assesses the marriage.

Here's what I want to say. Any time you want to walk out on me, I won't make any fuss. You can have the children, and I won't fight about it. That's my birthday present to you, before it's too late. And I have no plans for myself. I'm not trying to get out of this marriage, but you're forty now and you're entitled to whatever is left. (. . .)

I love you now, Bobbie, and I never used to. I guess you can't love anybody else while you have no self-respect. When the war was over I was sure I'd get the bounce at the plant, but they like me there, they've kept me on, and that one promotion. We'll never be back on Lantenengo Street, but I think I can count on a job here maybe the rest of my life. (. . .) I'll try, Bobbie. I've been trying. (. . .) How about you trying, too? (. . .) I'm not going to ask you who or when or any of that, but why is it you're faithful to me while I'm chasing after other women, and then when I'm faithful to you, you have somebody else? You're forty now and I'm forty-four. Let's see how long we can go without cheating?

Imagine Kissing Pete

John O'Hara

Short Story
M, 40s
Contemporary
Dramatic

1960. When Bobbie renews her on-again, off-again affair with Bill, he finds himself brimming with something "close to love."

You never forgot me. I never forgot you, either, Bobbie. I heard about you and Pete living in Fair Grounds. You know a couple times I took my car and dro' past your house to see which one it was. I didn't know, maybe you'd be sitting out on the front porch and if you saw me, you know. Maybe we just say hello and pass the time of day. But I didn't think no such thing, to tell you the God's honest truth. I got nothing against my wife, only she makes me weary. The house and the kids, she got me going to Mass every Sunday, all like that. But I ain't built that way, Bobbie. I'm the next thing to a hood, and you got that side of you, too. I'll make you any price you say, the other jerks you slept with, they never saw that side of you. You know, you hear a lot about love, Bobbie, but I guess I came closer to it with you than any other woman I ever knew. I never forgot you any more than you ever forgot me.

Imagine Kissing Pete
John O'Hara

Short Story
M, 40s
Contemporary
Dramatic

1960. Bill considers making an "honest woman" of Bobbie.

I'll be honest with you. Many's the time in bed with my wife I used to say to myself, "Peggy, you oughta take lessons from Bobbie McCrea." But who can give lessons huh? (. . .) How do you think I look? *(He slaps his belly.)* You look good. You put on a little. What? Maybe six pounds? (. . .) But you got it distributed. In another year Peggy's gonna weigh a hundred and fifty pounds, and I told her, I said either she took some of that off or I'd get another girl. Her heighth, [*sic*] you know. She can't get away with that much weight. I eat everything, but I do a lot of walking and standing. I guess I use up a lot of excess energy. Feel them muscles. Punch me in the belly. I got no fat on me anywhere, Bobbie. For my age I'm a perfect physical specimen. (. . .)

You know, the only thing I don't like about you, Bobbie, is the booze. If you'd lay off the sauce for a year I'd get rid of Peggy, and you and I could get married. But booze is women's weakness, [and] a female lush is the worst kind of a lush. (. . .)

[What,] you sore at me?

The Invisible Man

H. G. Wells

Novel
M, 30s
Classical
Dramatic

Griffin, the invisible man, reveals himself to Kemp.

I have had many adventures as an invisible man . . . but it is not going as I had planned. I am invisible only when I am undressed; with clothes on, I can be seen as easily as you. Do you know what it is like to run through the streets and fields on a night like this, without a stitch on one's back? (. . .) Ah yes, you nod your head. I had not thought the thing through, I confess. (. . .) But there are disadvantages, I can tell you. I cannot rest until I am sure that no one will discover me. I cannot eat unless I am alone, for I would be found out by the spoon floating in mid-air. In short, I am confounded at every turn. Dogs nip at me; they pick up my scent, even if they don't see me. There is no end of trouble. That is why this is such a stroke of luck, my running into you. Just think, man. I need an accomplice. With you in on my secret, I can take refuge in your house. (. . .) I made a huge mistake, Kemp, in trying to carry the thing through alone. Alone, there is so little I can do. But with a confederate, a thousand things are possible!

Ivan Hackler

Zeb Scanlan

Short Story
M, 17
Contemporary
Dramatic

*Living in a far-future America, Ivan Hackler observes
the people around him as news of Earth's eminent
destruction spreads.*

[C]rime and looting has gone up 76 percent. Not a surprise since the only reason for it is that people are starting
to think, "hey, my life doesn't matter at all, none of our
lives do, so let's do as much crazy shit as possible since it
doesn't really matter!" Today I bought a smoothie in
lunch then threw it at the wall, the assistant principal
started yelling at me, but then I just explained to him how
it doesn't matter since the world is going to end soon. He
started crying and walked away. (. . .) Many people have
quit their jobs and started to actually enjoy life. Think
about that; the world is going to be destroyed, we're all
going to die at the same moment, and my neighbor and
79 percent of the people in the world are the happiest
they've ever been. I get all these percentages from the
news, mainly CNN; most other channels have stopped
broadcasting. Everyone is watching CNN, at least the
people who really care are, and I watch it because I'm at
home a lot. I don't have much to do. I could go and raid
the local Radio Shack or Target.
 . . . maybe I will.

A Lesson Before Dying

Ernest J. Gaines

Novel
M, 30s+
Contemporary
Dramatic

1940s Louisiana, Cajun Country. A young black man is on trial for his life. Here the defense attorney offers his racist argument for the young man's innocence.

Gentlemen of the jury, look at this—this—this boy. I almost said man, but I can't say man. Oh, sure, he has reached the age of twenty-one, when we, civilized men, consider the male species has reached manhood, but would you call this—this—this a man? No, not I. I would call it a boy and a fool. A fool is not aware of right and wrong. A fool does what others tell him to do. A fool got into that automobile. A man with a modicum of intelligence would have seen that those racketeers meant no good. But not a fool. A fool got into that automobile. A fool rode to the grocery store. A fool stood by and watched this happen, not having the sense to run.

Gentlemen of the jury, look at him—look at him—look that this. Do you see a man sitting here? I ask you, I implore, look carefully—do you see a man sitting here?

A Lesson Before Dying
Ernest J. Gaines

Novel
M, 30s+
Contemporary
Dramatic

*1940s Louisiana, Cajun Country. A young black man
is about to be convicted and go to the electric
chair for murder. Here the defense attorney offers his
racist argument for the young man's innocence.*

Look at the shape of this skull, this face as flat as the
palm of my hand—look deeply into those eyes. Do you
see a modicum of intelligence? Do you see anyone here
who could plan a murder, a robbery, (. . .) can plan anything? A cornered animal to strike quickly out of fear, a
trait inherited from his ancestors in the deepest jungle of
blackest Africa—yes, yes, that he can do—but to plan? To
plan, gentlemen of the jury? No, gentlemen, this skull
here holds no plans. What you see here is a thing that
acts on command. A thing to hold the handle of a plow, a
thing to load your bales of cotton, a thing to dig your
ditches, to chop your wood, to pull your corn. That is
what you see here, but you do not see anything capable of
planning a robbery or a murder. (. . .) Ask him to name
the months of the year. Ask him does Christmas come before or after the Fourth of July? Mention the names of
Keats, Byron, Scott, and see whether the eyes will show
one moment of recognition. (. . .) Gentlemen of the jury,
this man planned a robbery? Oh, pardon me, pardon me,
I surely did not mean to insult your intelligence by saying
"man"—would you please forgive me for committing
such an error???

Marjorie Daw
Thomas Bailey Aldrich

Short Story
M, 20s-30s
Classical
Comic

1873. Edward Delany rejects the worthy Miss Daw.

You ask me why I do not fall in love with [Miss Daw.] I
will be frank, Jack; I have thought of that. She is young,
rich, accomplished, uniting in herself more attractions,
mental and personal, than I can recall in any girl of my
acquaintance; but she lacks the something that would be
necessary to inspire in me that kind of interest. Possessing
this unknown quantity, a woman neither beautiful nor
wealthy nor very young could bring me to her feet. But
not Miss Daw. If we were shipwrecked together on an un-
inhabited island—let me suggest a tropical island, for it
costs no more to be picturesque—I would build her a
bamboo hut, I would fetch her breadfruit and cocoanuts,
I would fry yams for her, I would lure the ingenuous turtle and make her nourishing soups, but I wouldn't make
love to her—not under eighteen months. I would like to
have her for a sister, that I might shield her and counsel
her, and spend half my income on thread-laces and
camel's-hair shawls. (We are off the island now.) If such
were not my feeling, there would still be an obstacle to
my loving Miss Daw. A greater misfortune could scarcely
befall me than to love her. I am about to make a revelation
that will astonish you. I may be all wrong in my premises
and consequently in my conclusions; but you shall judge.

Marjorie Daw

Thomas Bailey Aldrich

Short Story
M, 20s-30s
Classical
Seriocomic

1873. And why does Edward Delany reject the worthy Miss Daw? He explains to his friend, Flemming.

You ask me why I do not fall in love with [Miss Daw]. (. . .)

I am about to make a revelation that will astonish you. I may be all wrong in my premises and consequently in my conclusions; but you shall judge. (. . .)

I have seen Miss Daw perhaps ten times, and on each occasion I found that when I was not speaking of you or your sister, or some person or place associated with you, I was not holding her attention. Her eyes would wander away from me to the sea, or to some distant object in the landscape her fingers would play with the leaves of a book in a way that convinced me she was not listening. At these moments if I abruptly changed the theme—I did it several times as an experiment—and dropped some remark about my friend Flemming, then the somber blue eyes would come back to me instantly.

As for myself, all other things being favorable, it would be impossible for me to fall in love with a woman who listens to me only when I am talking of my friend!

The More I Like Flies

Reginald McKnight

Short Story
M, 30+
Contemporary
Dramatic

A kitchen worker muses on a coworker's loaded question.

(. . .) and then, like, from nowhere ol' Kelly goes, "What's so great about bein' goddamn white?" Hello! I say to myself. There he goes. Good ol' Kelly. But I keep my mouth shut, naturally. No sense going into it. (. . .)

But still, I'm thinking, How about this, ya dope: Try walking down the street at night, minding your own beeswax, and a white couple comes at you from the opposite way? and it's hot outside, so you're ambling, just ambling, and it's not all that late, just blue black with a few stars, like you like it, and you're thinking about, say, nothing really, OK? and you don't even mind the water sprinklers spitting on your right side. And the crickets sound nice, don't they? Then when Ken and Barbie get within a half block of you they cut across the street like you're a hissing viper hell hound man, bristling with Uzis and hypodermic needles. You can barely keep yourself from hollering. *Oh, come ooonnn. I gotta Korean girlfriend and my best buddy's white, and you people got to simply lay off watching so many goddamn drug lord movies.* Weenies. What's so great about being white is you get to act like everybody else in the world is a scary monster.

The Most Dangerous Game

Richard Connell

Short Story
M, 40s
Contemporary
Dramatic

In this widely anthologized short story, General Zaroff explains to Rainsford the rules of the hunt, in which Rainsford is to be the human prey.

I have but one passion in my life, Mr. Rainsford, and it is the hunt. (. . .) It would be impossible for me to tell you how many animals I have killed. (. . .) On this island, I hunt more dangerous game. (. . .) May I pour you another glass of port, Mr. Rainsford? (. . .)

I wanted the ideal animal to hunt, so I said: "What are the attributes of an ideal quarry?" And the answer was, of course: "It must have courage, cunning, and, above all, it must be able to reason." (. . .)

Tonight, we will hunt—you and I. (. . .)

Ivan will supply you with hunting clothes, food, a knife. I suggest you wear moccasins; they leave a poorer trail. I suggest too that you avoid the big swamp in the southeast corner of the island. There's quicksand there. One foolish fellow tried it. The deplorable part of it was that Lazarus followed him. You can imagine my feelings, Mr. Rainsford. I loved Lazarus; he was the finest hound in my pack. Well, I must beg you to excuse me now. I always take a siesta after lunch. You'll want to start, no doubt. I shall not follow till dusk. Hunting at night is so much more exciting than by day, don't you think? Au revoir, Mr. Rainsford, au revoir.

Mouth Hole

Wendi Aarons

Blog Entry
M, 30+
Contemporary
Comic

Dad melts down.

Oh, my God, I was right! What is it? Is it a tumor? A hole? It IS a hole! I knew it! How the hell did he get a hole on the roof of his mouth? Has he been eating chemicals? Did he drink the Febreze? Because that stuff kind of smells appetizing, don't you think? It's like fruit cake in a spray! In fact, sometimes I even think about licking the couch after I've sprayed it, ~~but only when I have low blood sugar~~ and . . . do you think it's congenital? Do you think it's something his dentist should have noticed? This is horrible! We should call 911. Should we call 911? Let's call 911. No! Let's just go directly to the ER. We can take my car—I just got gas, which by the way, was $3.00 a damn gallon, can you believe . . . suitcase. I should take a suitcase, right? Do you think this means he needs surgery? Does it mean he has a disease? Does it mean he can spit out of his nose, because at least that'd get him on TV, well, reality TV, but . . .

Um, what? [It's broccoli?]

Oh. Ha! That's funny, isn't it?

OK, it's not. But look on the bright side—at least we know he's eating his vegetables! Right? Right? Where are you going?

My Father's Girlfriend

Irene Ziegler

Novel
M, 55
Contemporary
Dramatic

Ed Bartlett dumps his mistress, Florida, who has just called him a coward.

I'm a lot of things, Florida: a liar, a cheat, a drunk, bad father, bad husband, bad excuse for a human being, but I am not a coward. A coward would run from a woman trying to turn him against his own blood. It takes a particular kind of bravery to love you in spite of your meanness and greed, but I did it, because, unlike a lot of men who try to hook themselves to your garters, I saw more than a bottled blonde with her own bank account. I saw a successful, independent businesswoman—full of piss and vinegar—who liked to make me laugh. You made me remember what it was like to wake up and look forward to the rest of the day.

But I don't feel any love coming back to me, Florida. You talk about our future, but you're doing everything you can to wipe out my past. You want me to sell my house to a man who will pull it down. You want me to turn my back on one daughter and ignore the other. Here I got a good woman up to the house who knows I'm cheatin' on her. Ever' night this week, I've listened to her rant and rave and cry herself to sleep, just so I can sneak a little slap and tickle after you're through serving watered-down, overpriced hooch to good people who deserve better. I gotta ask myself what the hell I'm doin'. I can't turn my life upside-down for a woman only interested in what she wants. I'm too old for that shit. From now on, I don't want to hear another word about my house, my family, or my cowardliness. I'm done talkin' about it. We're through.

My Kid's Dog

Ron Hansen

Short Story
M, 35+
Contemporary
Comic

Some people just aren't "dog people."

My kid's dog died.

Sparky.

I hated that dog.

The feeling was mutual.

We got off on the wrong foot. Whining in his pen those first nights. My squirt gun in his face and him blinking from the water. And then the holes in the yard. The so-called accidents in the house. His nose snuffling into my Brooks Brothers trousers. Him slurping my fine Pilsner beer or sneaking bites of my Dagwood sandwich when I fell asleep on the sofa. Also his inability to fetch, to take a joke, to find the humor in sudden air horns. To be dandled, roughhoused, or teased. And then the growling, the skulking, the snapping at my ankles, the hiding from me under the house, and literally thousands of abject refusals to obey. Like, *Who the hell are you?*

You'd have thought he was a cat.

The New Age and You and A Very Real Place Called Hell

Zev Borow

Online Journal Entry
M, 20s-30s
Contemporary
Comic

What do you like about the pope?

Me? What do I like about the pope? Lots of things. Like, say the two of you are having drinks and everyone starts talking about something a little, well . . . controversial: hip hop, abortion, the designated hitter, whatever. You know how it is; there are some people who don't want to go there. They'll be all like "whoa, let's not go there," and then maybe chuckle or do an impression. Not the pope. The pope goes there. He tells you what he thinks. In a nice way, too. And he'll surprise you. Like we were out with a bunch of people, and it's getting a little late, and everyone's having a good time, and I just happen to be sitting right next to the pope, to his left. But it's not like I really know him that well so it's a little, I don't know, weird. I mean this is a powerful person, leader of the Catholic church, a guy who wears robes. Anyway, things are wrapping up, the check is on the table, and he leans over to me and says, "Hey, Zev, I have a question for you." I was just psyched he remembered my name. "Hit me," I say, and he goes and does the thing where he raises his hand and makes like he's gonna hit me. Funny.

Notes from the Underground

Fydor Dostoevsky, Translator Constance Garnett

Novel
M, 20s
Classical
Dramatic

The Underground Man is a bitter, misanthropic man living alone in St. Petersburg, Russia, in the 1860s. A veteran of the Russian civil service, he holds an antagonistic position toward society.

As soon as I go in I'll give it him. Ought I before giving him the slap to say a few words by way of preface? No. I'll simply go in and give it him. They will all be sitting in the drawing room, and he with Olympia on the sofa. That damned Olympia! She laughed at my looks on one occasion and refused me. I'll pull Olympia's hair, pull Zverkov's ears! No, better one ear, and pull him by it round the room. Maybe they will all begin beating me and will kick me out. That's most likely, indeed. No matter! Anyway, I shall first slap him; the initiative will be mine (. . .). He will be forced to fight. And let them beat me now. Let them, the ungrateful wretches! Trudolyubov will beat me hardest, he is so strong; Ferfitchkin will be sure to catch hold sideways and tug at my hair. But no matter, no matter! That's what I am going for. The blockheads will be forced at last to see the tragedy of it all! When they drag me to the door I shall call out to them that in reality they are not worth my little finger. It's settled then—we shall fight at daybreak.

oldsmobile

Clay McLeod Chapman

Short Story
M, 60+
Contemporary
Dramatic

A husband finds in his wife's deteriorating state of mind a way to relive their past.

Alzheimer's has given me back my wife. She's twenty-three years old today. We're on our honeymoon all over again, heading west along Interstate 40—the rattle of tin cans tied to the rear bumper trailing in our wake, clattering across the asphalt. There's a bed and breakfast waiting for us in the California panhandle, only forty-five years away. We'll reach it within a few bends of the cerebellum. Until then it's just Lela and me and the open road. The wind's ironing out the wrinkles in her face, leaving her looking as young as the day when we first took this trip.

How old we really are doesn't matter anymore. It's all new to her now. We're on a never-ending road trip, where every bend brings back another memory of who she was.

If I can just keep her in the car, driving her Alzheimer's in circles, then I can keep Lela from forgetting where we first fell in love.

We have a full tank of gas. The radio's turned on and the volume's up as high as it'll go. The windows are all rolled down. The wind is everywhere.

The road is ours.

Only Twice I've Wished For Heaven

Dawn Turner Trice

Short Story
M, 45+
Contemporary
Dramatic

*Convinced they must move to a better neighbor-
hood, a father must now persuade his reluctant
young daughter.*

You haven't heard one word, have you, honey? (. . .)

There was a time, when I first met your mama, that I
would never have even considered living among the
"bourgeoisie." But there comes a time when you have to
mix some ideas. You get older and understand that nothing is all good; nothing is all bad. You know why I decided to go back to school? I wanted to give you
somebody who does more than drive a cab, and write letters to newspapers and hand out pamphlets in his spare
time. I had to ask myself, What more could I offer my
wife, my daughter? In a few months, you'll be twelve
years old. Soon, you'll be going off to college. I want you
to be proud of where you come from and I want you to
be proud of me. I'll be a teacher, honey. Your old man a
teacher at a fine, fine school.

Oreo

Everett T. Burnett

Novel
M, 45-50
Contemporary
Dramatic

*Clay Booker, an African-American businessman, is
determined to go forward with a major deal de-
spite criticism from his partner and people within
their community. He is talking to his partner, Winton.*

Did you know that at one time, Henry Ford offered a
deal to George Washington Carver? Oh yeah! (. . .)

You know why Carver turned down Ford's offer?
Ford was a rabid racist. Carver's patents all went to the
government. What a goddamned waste. Sure, Ford was
racist, but he recognized talent. He recognized opportunity and that's all Carver was for him, an opportunity. By
all accounts, he hated black people, but he was willing to
subsidize the work of a black man, because of the merit
of that man's work. That is all that we or any minority
can ask of anyone. It was Carver that needed to get past
his problem with racism, his inferiority complex. He
should have used Ford just as Ford was using him.

We're not going the way of that Uncle Tom, Carver.
We're making this deal. This would mean too much to
the community, to black Americans at large. When you
come to the office on Monday, when those Chrysler people are here, you leave your "steppinfetchit, let's make the

white folks apologize" attitude at the door. When you come in here, you think of your family and your community; and whether you want black Americans to still be the underclass of this country a hundred years from now.

Oreo
Everett T. Burnett

Novel
M, 45-50
Contemporary
Dramatic

*Clay Booker, an African-American businessman, is
determined to go forward with a major deal de-
spite criticism from his partner and people within
their community. He is talking to his partner, Winton.*

Did you know that at one time, Henry Ford offered a
deal to George Washington Carver? Oh yeah! Henry Ford
was gonna set Carver up with a lab and a marketing team
to sell new products, the way major corporations do
today. Carver had already founded Tuskegee. Ford was
offering to subsidize Tuskegee Institute's "new technology
division" for a mere share of the profit. Carver would
have kept all the patents.

What would have happened if he left his peanut
patents to the Tuskegee Institute? Do you realize that the
process to make peanut butter is the same process they
use to turn polyurethane into plastic? What if that process
belonged to an all-black university as early as the turn of
the twentieth century?

People the world over would be coming to the
Tuskegee Institute in Alabama. It would have become one
of the leading academic institutes in the world, not just "a
good black school." There would be blacks in the inner
sanctum of American plutocracy. (. . .)

We're not going the way of that Uncle Tom, Carver.
We're making this deal.

The Other Side of Air

Jeanne Braselton

Novel
M, 80s
Contemporary
Seriocomic

Ephraim resists his son and daughter-in-law's attempts to move him to Florida.

What would make you think I'd leave my life to go live in a concrete village with you and some damn strangers to be treated with this kind of disrespect? (. . .) You're stupider than I thought you were if you've spent more than the duration of an hour-long drunk considering it. (. . .) Amazed me, too, the other Christmas at your house, Anne, when your father took a drink and told me he felt like he'd been bound, gagged, and shoved in the trunk so he could be taken to Miami Beach and forced to live piddling around a concrete-block village because his wife was tired of looking fat in winter clothes. He told me not to tell anybody, but under the circumstances, I think he'd want me to.

A Piece of Cake

Robert Crisman

Novel
M, 30s
Contemporary
Dramatic

*Eddie is a small-time crook who is telling his crime
partner what he'd like to do with his share of the
money they figure is coming from their
planned heist.*

You know, Dennis—you'll laugh, man, but—what I'd really like to do is open a bookstore.

That place I was at, Cedar Creek? They had this library there, man, just off the dayroom, an' we come home after slavin' all day in the woods an' that's right where I'd head.

Nobody around, just me. An' all the noise an' the bullshit, just, way far away . . . An' I use to think, you know, if I had to make a livin'? I'd be, I'd like to just, be in a room like that, snuggled up in my chair, fire in the grate, rain howlin' outside, they're marchin' to war in Lower Slobbovia an' who gives a fuck?

Check it out. It's like, you ain't out there rippin' an' runnin', just waitin' to get your ass hauled off to jail. An' you *ain't* humpin' ass nine-to-five at some borin'-ass bullshit to make rent an' eat. *Fuck* all that noise. My old man got laid off at Todd's in '72. Couldn't get no job. Then he started back drinkin'. Come '77 he's dead of cirrhosis. It ain't gonna happen to me.

I dunno, man, just, we do this, I get where I'm goin' an' so forth an', fuck it. I mean, just lemme pay my taxes, you know? Have enough left over for a roof an' a cot an' a car, an' every so often a nice, juicy steak, an' I'm cool. Maybe sometime meet some nice chick, pretty face an' a cute little ass, I can talk to an' stuff . . . come home an' get belly to belly . . . that's all I want, really, no shit. I'd even get out an' vote for the crooks they got runnin' for office they let me. Citizen Ryan. My little slice of American Pie, you know what I'm sayin'.

That's what I want.

A Play
Bruce Morrow

Short Story
M, 25+
Contemporary
Dramatic

A black gay man imagines himself on stage, in the terrifying solo show that is his life.

No one's clapping. The stage lights are up and no one's clapping. There wasn't any music either. There should have been music before the lights. Dueling guitars, drums beating, never settling in one time signature. (. . .) Then the lights should have slowly risen. (. . .)

There's a commotion in the audience, muted voices, squabble, like two trumpets competing for the final solo. Two trumpets. One, my father stuttering the same phrase over and over again: Fucking faggot. Fucking faggot. Fucking faggot. The other, my mother shushing, her teeth together, her fingers to her lips, puckered. Shushing as she stands to Dad's command, his one hand on her elbow, the other holding an empty glass. She's fumbling for her coat and purse, trying not to let her eyes leave the stage. I can feel her eyes on me. Smack some sense into me. Knock the color off my skin. One more time. Don't see me. Dad, one more time, the bruises, the black eyes, the nose bleeds. Fucking faggot is all that he sees on this stage and he isn't turning around as he pushes Momma out the door.

I can see them clearly in the light of the theater's outer lobby, framed in the doorway. I'm not a part of them any-more. I'm not myself anymore. For two weeks, the time it takes to get my test results back, I will be on this stage, I will be a number, #000, triple naught. Negative, I hope. Going over every aspect of my life, every sexual encounter, every slap across my face, every heartbreak, every freckle on my skin.

Please Take
Jason Roeder

Online Journal Entry
M, 25+
Contemporary
Comic

Please take my couch. There's not a thing wrong with it, but the doorways in my new place are far too narrow to accommodate it. Take the air conditioner, too. It's perfect for a small apartment. It rattles and leaks a little, and I've lost all the window brackets, but it'll do the job come August.

This bookcase is yours for the asking. The front corner kind of slumps, so you'll have to devote at least one of your books to propping it up. (. . .)

My shower massager isn't going to fit on the spout in my new place, so you might as well have it. (. . .) The "Standard" setting essentially simulates your existing water pressure, just in case you enjoy the sensation of having thrown your money away. The "Massage" setting (. . .) at some point it was actually cannibalized by the next setting, "Bruise." (. . .) The last setting has no name. The water simply explodes from the open jaws of a skull. If I've used it, I have no memory of the event.

You'll love this microwave oven. (. . .) I'm not sure what I did, but the turntable has precisely adjusted its rotation speed to match that of the planet Venus. Be aware that it will take almost a year for your pizza rolls to make the full trip around, and plan your Super Bowl party accordingly.

I'd love to offer you this ice-cream maker. But, deep down, I know it will never let me go.

Private First Class
Reginald "Malik" Edwards

Wallace Terry

Oral History
M, 30+
Contemporary
Dramatic

Originally from Louisiana, Edwards served as a rifle-man in the 9th Regiment of the U.S. Marine Corps in Danang, June 1965–March 1966.

The first thing happened to me, I looked out and here's a bamboo snake. That little short snake, the one that bites you and you're through bookin'. What do you do when a bamboo snake comin' at you? You drop your rifle with one hand, and shoot his head off. You don't think you can do this, but you do it. So I'm so rough with this snake, everybody thinks, well, Edwards is shootin' his ass off today.

So then this old man runs by. This other sergeant says, "Get him, Edwards." But I missed the old man. Now I just shot the head off a snake. You dig what I'm sayin'? Damn near with one hand. M-14. But all of a sudden, I missed this old man. 'Cause I really couldn't shoot him.

So Brooks—he's got the grenade launcher—fired. Caught my man as he was comin' through the door. But what happened was it was a room full of children. Like a schoolroom. And he was runnin' back to warn the kids that the Marines were coming. And that's who got hurt. All those little kids and people.

The Pursuer
Julio Cortázar, Translator Paul Blackburn

Short Story
M, 35+
Contemporary
Dramatic

Johnny Carter, modeled after jazz musician Charlie Parker, explains how music helped him cope with his tumultuous childhood.

I remember when I was just a kid, almost as soon as I'd learned to play sax. There was always a helluva fight going on at home, and all they ever talked about was debts and mortgages. You know what a mortgage is? It must be something terrible, because the old lady blew her wig every time the old man mentioned mortgage, and they'd end up in a fistfight. I was thirteen then . . . but you already heard all that. (. . .)

Because of the way things were at home, time never stopped, dig? From one fistfight to the next, almost not stopping for meals. And to top it all off, religion, aw, you can't imagine. When the boss got me a sax, you'd have laughed yourself to death if you'd seen it, then I think I noticed the thing right off. Music got me out of time, but that's only a way of putting it. If you want to know what I think, really, I believe that music put me *into* time.

Random Spam
Anonymous

Found Text
M/F, 20+
Contemporary
Comic

From a random, spam e-mail promoting undervalued stock, this text struck us as bizarrely performable. Maybe.

The Scooby snack teaches the tornado. Any lover can share a shower with the cloud formation inside the tomato, but it takes a real recliner to bury the moldy globule. A tape recorder seeks a sandwich. When you see the ski lodge, it means that the tattered customer goes to sleep. The underhandedly fractured mortician secretly plans an escape from a near industrial complex, and the plaintiff from the cashier makes love to a carelessly nuclear tape recorder.

Now and then, a briar patch goes deep sea fishing with a nation from a rattlesnake. Any oil filter can compete with some scythe, but it takes a real pit viper to ridiculously bestow great honor upon a mastadon. When a nuclear customer is paternal, the flatulent avocado pit lazily recognizes a vaporized cowboy. Most people believe that some turkey single-handedly secretly admires a mortician, but they need to remember how single-handedly a self-actualized avocado pit returns home.

Rat Bohemia

Sarah Schulman

Novel
M, 30s
Contemporary
Seriocomic

David, a writer with HIV, finds his parents infuriating.

The phone has been ringing all day. They keep ringing
and hanging up. Ringing and hanging up. I know who it
is. It is my mother. My parents are trying to kill me.

They don't call regularly. They call on a whim. They
might be sitting around the house one Sunday afternoon,
breakfast is done. The paper is done. Nothing to do for
an hour before taking in a movie. *Hey,* my mother will
think to herself. *I just remembered that I have a son.*

How do I know this? It's because they never call on a
Friday night. They never, never call from nine to five.
They never sit down and write a letter. It is just here and
there during their occasional free time. So, during the
workday I can answer the phone but, between seven and
nine on weekend mornings I have to let the machine get
it. I couldn't bear to actually talk to one of them. The casual indifference would shatter me. I can't take one more
act of unlove.

Rat Bohemia

Sarah Schulman

Novel
M, 30s
Contemporary
Seriocomic

David, a writer with HIV, finds his parents infuriating.

That's when I realized that my parents were trying to kill me. In fact, my entire family is in on it. Their plan is to invite me in and throw me out. Invite me in and throw me out, invite me in and throw me out until I have gone completely insane and hang myself in my own bedroom. It is their only possible motive.

Here's one of their favorite tactics for driving me insane. My mother likes to call me up and leave messages about obscure elderly relatives who have died, asking me to attend their funerals. She usually calls after we haven't seen each other for a year or two, asking me to show up at a gathering of relatives knowing that it would be the site of our first reunion. Does that sound appropriate? Does that sound like someone who really wants to see me?

The Remains of Crazy Horse

Douglas Schnitzspahn

Short Story
M, 30+
Contemporary
Dramatic

The voice of a Native American speaks to The Tourist.

Maybe you have been to Yellowstone National Park before. (. . .) And, of course, you went to the Falls, Yellowstone Falls, dropping down into the sulfur cliffs of the Grand Canyon of the Yellowstone. You snapped pictures. You kissed your wife, on the cheek. You yelled at your kids when they stuck their heads through the railing. (. . .)

You never knew what happened here before all the railings though. This place had no name then (. . .) melded into other land, into prairies, back up into mountains, off to the ocean, drained into rivers. A group of Indians ran here. Soldiers walked through their teepees at night, shooting indiscriminately. The Indians regrouped, butchered them, cut off their balls and stuffed them into their mouths. More soldiers came. The women and children, the old and the ones who no longer wanted to fight, left for the reservations. But the warriors ran. None of the interpretive signs tell you how they ran here, how the soldiers followed.

The Remains of Crazy Horse
Douglas Schnitzspahn

Short Story
M, 20s-30s
Contemporary
Dramatic

In the shadow of the unfinished monument to Crazy Horse, Tyler speaks to Peter, an older white man with considerable white guilt and a somewhat romanticized view of Native American culture.

I'm only half Indian, man, the fucked-up half. Besides I don't believe in all that bullshit. It's all just some crap a bunch of rich white people in California pay a lot of money for. No one believes in that Indian stuff. (. . .)

You got a light? (. . .) (*Offering a smoke.*) You know, peace pipe?

(. . .) I don't think it ever existed, a peaceful place. (. . .) My grandmother believes in all that medicine man stuff. She told me once that the Lakota all used to live underground. She said that when they finally wandered up to the earth, they started to change, that half of them became humans and half turned into buffalo. She says that the Indians and the buffalo and all the animals used to live together as one people.

(. . .) You're nuts, old man.

Scorched Earth

David L. Robbins

Novel
M, 20+
Contemporary
Dramatic

Elijah, a young black man married to a white woman, is in jail. He is accused of burning a church because parishioners dug up his dead baby when he and his wife, Clare, buried her in the white cemetery. Elijah talks to his attorney.

You believe what you want. But I didn't burn that church. (. . .)

You should have seen what they did. What they did to Nora Carol. And to Clare. She, um . . . she wouldn't cry. She just kept saying how stupidity and hate were just part of the world, you know, and we'd been lucky so far to have as little of it come our way as we did. Even after giving birth to Nora Carol and having her be the way she was, you know, even after going through that two days before, Clare was . . . she just wouldn't cry. She kept telling me all morning, Elijah, it ain't us, it's them. We're not the ones doing this, they are. We didn't dig up a baby, we didn't do anything unjust. She said maybe that's why God took Nora Carol from us. To show everybody what's going on, that there's still so much hate out there. Maybe it was time folks saw into their own hearts. Maybe that's what this is all about.

Mr. Deeds, you gonna talk to Clare? Will you do me a favor when you do? Tell her this is all going to be OK. Even if you don't think it is. Do that for me.

Scorched Earth
David L. Robbins

Novel
M, 30+
Contemporary
Dramatic

An infant of mixed race has been buried in a white cemetery. Mr. Quantrill, a church-going man, makes his case for exhuming the infant and burying her in the black cemetery.

You know, pastor, I hate to say it. But you look outside these windows here and you see a world we built with our fathers and their fathers and on before them, and that world is getting smaller every day. Today we got quotas and affirmative action and set-asides. (. . .) You got black farmer's associations and black businessmen's associations and black congressional caucuses. And we don't argue, we don't oppose 'em, we even help 'em along when we can. Back a hundred and forty years ago, a bunch of folks out there in the graveyard started a black Baptist church up the road so's the blacks could have their own private place of worship and their own cemetery, so's they could worship and be buried among their own.

So I got to ask you, pastor. How much smaller is our world going to get? Is it so small now that we can't even lay our heads down together with the folks we come up with? Do we have to throw open every door? I like Elijah, by God I do, but that don't mean I want to be buried with him or his kin. That poor little baby ought to be laid to rest in a place surrounded by her own people, and that place isn't here, it's up the road. I don't believe it's a sin to want that for her, or to want the same for me, or these good folks here with me tonight. I just don't.

Self-Sabotage

Matthew Ivan Bennett

Journal Entry
M, 20s-30s
Contemporary
Comic

An intelligent man struggles with self-loathing and unemployment.

It took me filling out a job application for McDonald's before I fully awoke to the Manichean dualism inside me. Remember the cartoons—the red devil on one shoulder, the pussy angel on the other? Not what I'm talking about. That's a retarded simplification; the CNN version of the Deep Throat, Orwellian, Bobby-Fisher-versus-the-Rusky crap that plays out inside of me. I mean, do I want to work at McDonald's? Uh, no. Who wants to turn already processed food into thoroughly processed food? Not on my list of things. I was there, drum roll, because I hate myself. I grease the ring of self-actualization because the tiniest tactile contact with success scares the poop out of me. But! While I was there, filling out the app, I recognized it—and in an act of self-respect I walked out, crossed the street, and I filled out an application for Burger King instead. I mean, at least they flame-broil.

Sonnet CXXXVIII
William Shakespeare

Poem
M, 40+
Classical
Seriocomic

Lovers flatter with mutual lies.

When my love swears that she is made of truth
I do believe her, though I know she lies,
That she might think me some untutor'd youth,
Unlearned in the world's false subtleties.
Thus vainly thinking that she thinks me young,
Although she knows my days are past the best,
Simply I credit her false-speaking tongue:
On both sides thus is simple truth suppress'd.
But wherefore says she not she is unjust?
And wherefore say I not that I am old?
O, love's best habit is in seeming trust,
An age in love loves not to have years told:
  Therefore I lie with her and she with me,
  And in our faults by lies we flatter'd be.

A Special Message from The American Fruit Company

Greg Machlin

Poem
M, 20s-40s
Contemporary
Comic

Frank is a marketing executive at the American Fruit Company. He likes his job.

I do marketing for the American Fruit Company:
"We believe in fruit."
Say you're someone who doesn't like . . . bananas.
I like bananas.
You can peel them,
eat bite-size chunks
No juice—
It's the *neatest* fruit you'll ever eat!
But you don't like 'em.

So I order a "Code Orange."
Late that night, our special ops team goes into your house
so quiet,
You're snorin' like a baby,
They peel back your sheets and
Slap a bunch of banana stickers on your butt!

Next morning. "What're these banana stickers doin' on
my butt?"

As you painfully rip them off,
you might think,
"Gee! Maybe I should stop my senseless BANANA-
boycott!
And have a freakin' banana!"

That's a Code Orange. You don't want to see a Code
Red.
Nobody does. I sure wish I hadn't.
It'll just be easier if, next time you're at the supermarket,
you buy a bunch of bananas!
We could even deliver them. On the House! Free of
charge!

And that's how we go the extra mile
to make sure you're eating your fruit.
Good evening, and God Bless America.

Stay Down
Tammy Peacy

Short Story
M, 55-65
Contemporary
Dramatic

A neighbor fears for the young woman next door.

This time must have been bad. I think they took her out in an ambulance.

I try not to intrude. Try not to be the nosy neighbor, but that girl is going to end up dead. She should take her kids and just get out of there. There are places she could go. Sure, she's probably scared, but she's got to think of those kids.

He knows it's me who keeps calling the police. When I'm out in the yard I see him sometimes, working on that snazzy truck of his. I don't bother with being neighborly at all. And he just looks at me like he could rip me apart on the spot. He's a big guy, he probably could. I don't let him intimidate me.

My sister tried leaving four, five times. But every time her husband would woo her on back. Promising it would never happen again, he loved her, blah, blah, blah. The whole "Prince Charming" act. That one, he wasn't even a drunk like this schmuck next door, he was just plain mean. My sister would have been forty-seven in a few months. My baby sister. She only got to see thirty-three years.

This girl over here, I wonder how old she is?

Tastes Like Chicken

R. T. Smith

Short Story
M, 45+
Contemporary
Seriocomic

A Virginia snake rancher shows off his menagerie to paying customers.

All these here behind the screen wire—look out!—are your eastern diamondbacks, *Crotalus horridus*, which are your most popular native snake, and as you see a little testy by nature. They've got the color pattern like Indian wampum or an hourglass, and those silver-looking noise-makers on the tail give 'em a musical impact, nodamean? Can't read the age by it, like some folks think, though. They'll not slough skin on any man's regular schedule. Woman's neither. Whoa back now. That's Darth, and the palish one twined with him is Michael for that Jackson freak on TV. One there giving us the hard eye is Hillary. (. . .) They're used to people, mostly. Still, you can't predict 'em. They can always marvel me, and everything they inspire I write down like their secretary. It's what you might call my passion, the scribbling. Some day, luck comes for me, I'll make a book and make a killing, downpay me a condo in some paradise. Jesse Turley's the name.

Thank You, Thank You, Thank You

Zev Borow

Op-Ed Contribution
M, 17
Contemporary
Comic

Upon being accepted to Yale, thanks are in order.

WOW! This is a huge surprise. I mean, I don't even remember applying to Yale. Kidding, kidding. So many people to thank; I don't even know where to begin. There's my whole team at Scarsdale High: my guidance counselor, Mr. Rondtree—Rondtree, you rock! My behavioral therapist since fifth grade, Mrs. Klein—we did it! It's not Harvard, but it's better than Syracuse! Of course, everyone on the Wampanoag Elder Council: Thank you for granting me tribal status and allowing me to claim Native American heritage on my application. I know my dad does a lot of legal work for you guys, but I'd like to think you consider me a real American Indian. Finally, I want to thank Dana Schwartz, and just as much, really, Dana's mom, Jocelyn, for letting Dana go to the prom with me even though she's a sophomore. Dana, even though you puked, you made that night very special, if you know what I mean, and I thank you for it.

War Is Kind

Stephen Crane

Poem
M, 20+
Classical
Dramatic

An ironic anti-war poem.

Do not weep, maiden, for war is kind.
Because your lover threw wild hands toward the sky
And the affrighted steed ran on alone,
Do not weep.
War is kind.

Hoarse, booming drums of the regiment
Little souls who thirst for fight,
These men were born to drill and die
The unexplained glory flies above them
Great is the battle-god, great, and his kingdom—
A field where a thousand corpses lie.

Do not weep, babe, for war is kind.
Because your father tumbled in the yellow trenches,
Raged at his breast, gulped and died,
Do not weep.
War is kind.

Swift, blazing flag of the regiment
Eagle with crest of red and gold,
These men were born to drill and die
Point for them the virtue of slaughter

Make plain to them the excellence of killing
And a field where a thousand corpses lie.

Mother whose heart hung humble as a button
On the bright splendid shroud of your son,
Do not weep.
War is kind.

The War of the Worlds

H. G. Wells

Novel
M, 30+
Classical
Dramatic

A soldier prepares to fight domination by Martians.

This isn't a war. It never was a war, any more than there's war between man and ants. (. . .) That's what we are now—just ants. (. . .) Here's intelligent things, and it seems they want us for food. First, they'll smash us up— ships, machines, guns, cities, all the order and organisation. All that will go. At present we're caught as we're wanted. A Martian has only to go a few miles to get a crowd on the run. And I saw one, one day, out by Wandsworth, picking houses to pieces and routing among the wreckage. But they won't keep on doing that. So soon as they've settled all our guns and ships, and smashed our railways, and done all the things they are doing over there, they will begin catching us systematic, picking the best and storing us in cages and things. (. . .) Lord! They haven't begun on us yet. Don't you see that? Cities, nations, civilisation, progress—it's all over. That game's up. We're beat. (. . .) Those who mean to escape their catching must get ready. I'm getting ready.

What You Know

Peter Ho Davies

Short Story
M, 30s
Contemporary
Dramatic

After an unspeakable tragedy in the high school where he teaches, a creative-writing teacher struggles to reconcile fiction and reality.

People suddenly want to know all about my students, what they're like. What do I know, I'm just a writer-in-the-schools. All I see is their writing. (. . .)

But most of the time I find myself telling them what not to write. All the narrative clichés. No stories about suicide. (. . .) "No suicides?" they say in the flat, whiny voices, as if there is nothing else, nothing better. "How can suicide be boring?"

Maybe not in life, I explain quickly, but in fiction? Sure. (. . .) "[Y]ou owe it to the material to do it justice, to find a way of making it real and raw for readers again."

They nod in complete incomprehension. (. . .) It's the nod you give a crazy man, a lunatic with a gun.

What really redeems it are the laughs. The laughable badness of their prose. (. . .) The cop slapping on the *cuff links*. The *viscous* criminal. The *escape* goat. (. . .)

So that, if you really want to know, is what my students are like. Does any of it explain why one of them last week shot his father in the head across the breakfast nook, rode the bus to school with pistol in his waistband, emptied it in his homeroom, killing two and wounding five, before putting the gun in his mouth and splashing his brains all over the whiteboard?

No stories about suicide? No viscous criminals?

When I Should Have Stopped Listening

Tim Cage

Short Story
M, 25+
Contemporary
Seriocomic

A man imagines speaking to a former boyfriend.

I listened to everything you said, without realizing that my listening had become memorizing. I listened, so I knew your birthday, your sister's name, the name of your cat that died while you were away at school. I amazed you by trotting out, weeks later, references to names and events you dropped casually. Birthday: October 4. Sister: Amanda. (. . .)

I listened because you were interesting, smart, and attractive. Also, I'd read somewhere that listening could make someone "wild about" you. I'd decided listening would be my secret weapon. I was wild about you, and needed something to make you wild about me.

During our final lunch, (. . .) I mustered the courage to tell you that I found you interesting and attractive. You said nothing. It never occurred to me that perhaps you hadn't been listening. So I asked if your interest in me had waned. You said that you were interested in me for all the same reasons I was interested in you. But. You said, "but."

It was hard to hear what you said next, because of my ego shattering. Shattering like a tray full of champagne glasses on a flagstone floor, all around my feet. You mentioned that this was a bad time, job stress, a lot on your mind, the holidays. All the while, I provided the requisite "uh-huhs" and bobbed my head, hoping that I looked more like someone nodding than drowning.

After our plates were cleared (. . .) you said, "Why don't we share a taxi back to mid-town?"

I swept up the shards of my ego and got with you into that taxi. I'll show you, I thought. I'll pick up the fare.

The Witch

Francine Prose

Short Story
M, 30s
Contemporary
Dramatic

*Zip and Jerry are cops. Zip responds to a call to
Jerry's house, and Jerry tells him his side of the story.*

I need to tell you something. (. . .) This is going to
sound crazy. But trust me on this. Marianne's a witch.
I *told* you, I know it sounds crazy, but I've seen her do
shit you wouldn't believe . . . Listen, the first time I met
her mother, this was back in Brooklyn, her mother tells
me that when Marianne was a kid, they'd go to
church (. . .) in the summer, a bunch of people would
faint, and it was always the people standing directly
around Marianne. And she always thought it *was* Marianne. Clearing herself some room. Her own *mom* tells me
this, and I don't listen! (. . .)

How do you think you got here tonight? Man, you
cannot believe how many guys get lost around here, the
FedEx man, the UPS man, the electric-meter reader,
they're always knocking on the door, Marianne's *bringing*
them up here, and I know it's just a matter of time before
one of them decides to stay. Or comes back. Or calls her.
And if she leaves, it'll kill me. I swear. (. . .)

All right. I'll let you go. Hey, man, listen. This is, like,
our little secret, right?

Young Goodman Brown

Nathaniel Hawthorne

Short Story
M, 20+
Classical
Dramatic

1835. A young Puritan man's illusions about the goodness of his society are crushed when he discovers that many of his fellow townspeople, including religious leaders and his wife, are attending a Black Mass. Here, the devil delights in revealing this awful truth.

Welcome, my children, to the communion of your race. Look behind you! There are all whom ye have reverenced from youth. Ye deemed them holier than yourselves, and shrank from your own sin, contrasting it with their lives of righteousness and prayerful aspiration heavenward. Yet here are they all in my worshipping assembly. This night it shall be granted you to know their secret deeds; how hoary-bearded elders of the church have whispered wanton words to the your maids of their households; how many a woman, eager for widows' weeds, has given her husband a drink at bedtime and let him sleep his last sleep in her bosom; how beardless youth have made hast to inherit their fathers' wealth; and how fair damsels—blush not, sweet ones—have dug little graves in the garden, and bidden me, the sole guest, to an infant's funeral. And now my children, look upon each other.

Lo, there thee stand, my children. Depending upon

one another's hearts, ye had still hope that virtue were not all a dream. Now are ye undeceived. Evil is the nature of mankind. Evil must be your only happiness. Welcome again, my children, to the communion of your race.

Your New Personal Trainer

By Jason Roeder

Online Journal Entry
M, 25+
Contemporary
Comic

My name's Jerry, and I'm going to show you around the Nautilus equipment. You had your eye on one of the other trainers, didn't you? That's OK. I don't mind being judged. In fact, once you get to know me, you'll realize just how generous your initial impression was . . .

I'm sorry, I was just thinking about how unappealingly hairy my forearms are. (. . .)

All right, let's get started. We don't have to make eye contact if you don't want to.

We'll begin with the leg press. It's good for overall lower-body strength, including the quads, the hamstrings, and the glutes. Oh, look at me with my little musculature shorthand—"glutes," "quads"—as if you can't see right through me, as if you don't know transparent insincerity when you hear it. That's why I'm not allowed to sell memberships anymore, you see. I always end up crying and eating ice cream in the middle of the pitch. Did you know I never sold a single membership, but somehow bought six? Anyway, I can tell by the way you're sipping from that bottle of Propel fitness water that you've already realized I don't have any authentic essence whatsoever.

Do three sets of ten. Feel the burn if you can feel anything.

MONOLOGUES BY AGE

MONOLOGUES BY TONE

COMIC MONOLOGUES

DRAMATIC MONOLOGUES

MONOLOGUES BY VOICE

MONOLOGUES BY AUTHOR

RIGHTS AND PERMISSIONS